# the Brownie

## Annual 1984

**Edited by
Penny Morris**

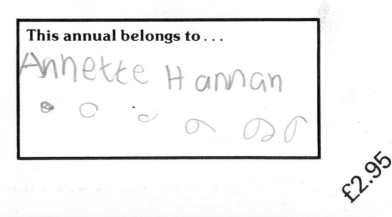

**This annual belongs to . . .**

Annette Hannan

£2.95

# MONKEY BUSINESS!

**photographs by Norman Redfern**

If ever you are on holiday in Cornwall, and you are going along a winding country lane just east of Looe, so narrow that two cars cannot pass, you may see a sign saying 'to the Monkey Sanctuary'.

If you follow the sign you will come to an even narrower, grassy lane sloping down towards the sea and there, in a hollow at the end of the lane, will be a large old house surrounded by rambling enclosures linked to the house and some magnificent beech trees, by a maze of walkways and ropes. This is the Looe Monkey Sanctuary and one autumn afternoon I went down there to meet the monkeys and some members of the 3rd Looe Brownie Pack.

The weather was rather stormy when we arrived and as the monkeys don't like rain they were sheltering inside the house. The Brownies however decided that they didn't mind the weather, and went out to meet some of the other animals who live at the Sanctuary.

As the weather didn't look as though it was going to improve, one of the helpers asked us if we would like to go inside the house to meet some of the monkeys in their 'lounge'.

When we were all settled around the room we were told a little about the Sanctuary and the monkeys we were going to meet.

The Sanctuary was started by Len Williams as a place for woolly monkeys to live and breed in a natural community. The monkeys originate from the Amazon region of South America and, although the weather here is obviously different, Mr Williams has tried to create a place where they can live as they would in the wild.

The oldest monkey, Lulu, is 27, and the only one that was not born in the Sanctuary.

Some of the older monkeys are grandparents. The monkeys become very attached to their families and are unhappy if for any reason they are separated.

The monkeys mainly eat fruit and vegetables, but they are also given meal-worms, moths, crickets, locusts and stick insects and, occasionally, a little bit of chicken or egg. They also like nuts and sunflower seeds, and even garlic! Visitors are not supposed to feed them and we were warned to keep any sweets or chocolates hidden as the monkeys would soon find them and help themselves if they got the chance!

We were asked not to grab at the monkeys when they came in as they don't like this. They enjoy being stroked and groomed, but not being held. While none of the monkeys has ever attacked anyone, some of the visitors have been told off by the monkeys for getting too familiar!

Several other animals live at the Sanctuary, including a large and friendly rabbit and a colony of North American prairie marmots living in burrows under the ground.

When Charlie sat on the Brownies he was surprisingly heavy, and they were impressed by the strength of his tail which he used to grip onto them. All the monkeys use their tails almost like a third arm, holding with them and swinging from them.

Sarah, one of the older females came in next, with her daughter Sophie. Like all the older monkeys, Sarah moved in a slow and dignified way and was not as playful as Charlie. Sophie, being quite young, preferred to stay near her mother.

**This is Sarah, one of the older monkeys, sitting with the Brownies.**

The first monkey to come into the lounge was Charlie. He was 2½ years old, which would be about 7 in human years. He was very quick and lively, leaping around the room and running along the floor in a game with the helper. He was also rather mischievous and investigated the Brownies' hats!

**Inside the house we were introduced to Charlie. Charlie was rather interested in the Brownies' hats, and after running off with one was made to hand it back.**

Some of the monkeys have learnt to use a cup and now prefer to drink this way. None has been trained or taught any tricks, everything they do they have learnt for themselves.

The monkeys are excellent climbers, using their tails to help them. They are not kept in enclosures all the time, but can climb out into the large trees near the house using ropes. None has ever tried to run away, because they regard the Sanctuary as their territory and feel safe living there among family and friends.

The Sanctuary is open to the public during the summer, except on Saturdays, and as well as the monkeys, there are marmots, macaws and donkeys to see.

Perhaps one day you will be able to visit the Sanctuary and meet the beautiful woolly monkeys of Looe!

# WANTED— ONE BROWNIE PACK

## by Verily Anderson

Illustrated by Jennifer Northway

"Quick, Lucy, look!" Tim gently shook awake his sister. "The sun rising over Africa!"

Lucy leant across from her seat in the aircraft to look through the small window which had been dark whenever she woke up in that long night in the air. Their Granny had seen the two of them off from England at dusk. Now Lucy could see a streak of orange light.

"Underneath us the clouds look like whipped up egg-whites when Mum's making meringues," Lucy said. "When we start to fly lower we might see elephants and wildebeests crowding round the water holes and maybe a lioness taking her cubs for a drink. It can't be long now before we land!"

But Joanna, the air hostess, who was keeping an eye on them, said first of all they must eat a big breakfast. She snapped open the folding tables attached to the backs of the seats in front of them, and put down a tray on each, its compartments loaded with little packages of butter and bread and cheese, sugar and salt and pepper, tiny cartons of marmalade and honey, as well as a plateful of hot sausages, tomatoes and bacon, and a cup for a hot drink.

"I can't eat all this!" Lucy exclaimed. "Can I take some of the packages home for my doll's house?"

"Of course you can," Joanna smiled. "I'll get you a bag."

But then Lucy remembered that they were not going home, and it would be two years, perhaps four, before she saw her doll's house again. By then the butter would have melted and the cheese gone mouldy and she would be too old to play with the doll's house. She told Tim about it.

"Take them all the same," he advised. "You can have most of mine too and share them out on a Brownie picnic."

"So Lucy's a Brownie?" Joanna had overheard him. "I was a Tawny Owl before I started flying. It was a good start for training to be an air hostess."

"I suppose it's not so very different," Lucy said. "Brownie Guiders and air hostesses both have to take care of a pack of people and keep them happy and cheerful for hours."

"Yes, and sometimes keep them quiet, too!" said Joanna. "Are you a Cub Scout, Tim?"

"Not yet," he said. "Maybe I will be in Africa."

"And I'm going to join another Pack when we get to the school up in the mountains where our parents are teachers," Lucy said. "I cut the sleeves off my Brownie uniform because I saw in a painting book that Brownies in Zimbabwe have short sleeves."

"And then Lucy made the cut-off sleeves into hand puppets for her Pack puppet show," said Tim.

"I made a Brown Owl puppet and a Tawny Owl puppet," Lucy explained.

When breakfast had been cleared away and Joanna had taken Lucy and Tim to wash and strip off some of their English winter clothes, they heard the pilot's voice hoping that everyone had enjoyed a comfortable flight. In twenty minutes they would be landing in Harare. Joanna came to see that their seat belts were fastened. Tim could not stop looking out of the window. He could see long winding rivers, and the roads, and then farms and then houses and then, seeming to move very fast towards them, the airfield itself, and — bump! — they felt the wheels touch the runway. It was an exciting moment!

"In a few minutes we'll be hugging Daddy," Tim said.

"And Mummy," Lucy added hopefully.

Joanna led them down the steps into the summery air of an early African morning. Inside the airport building she handed them over to their smiling parents and told them what easy passengers the children had been.

Soon Lucy and Tim were hauling their luggage up into the landrover that was used as a school bus. There were no windows at the back, so at first Lucy could not see the row of their new African schoolmates inside. Then, "Hello, Lucy! Hello, Tim!" they heard.

Except for a few monkeys in the trees and a baboon sitting by the roadside, Lucy and Tim could not see any of the wild animals they were looking for on their long rattling journey. The other children told them they would have to go to the game park several miles from the school to see more.

The last few miles were so bumpy they all tumbled about in the back, laughing. The bus crawled up the twisting track that eventually wound twice round the peak on which the school classrooms, dormitories and teachers' homes stood, beside the church, with higher mountains behind them.

What a long time ago that breakfast in the air seemed when Lucy and Tim had their next meal on the creeper-covered verandah of their new home! Once that was eaten they were ready to explore their home. They were to sleep in bunks under one green mosquito net.

"When you've had your rest," Mum said, "we'll all go for a swim in the school pool."

"We don't need a rest," Lucy assured her. "I want to practise for my Swimmer Badge. I can do the 25 metres all right, but I haven't tried picking up a plate from the bottom yet."

"Everybody has a rest here in the afternoon," Mum said. "We were all up early today and school starts at 7 o'clock every morning."

No sooner had Lucy climbed up into her bunk than she was sound asleep. When she woke she could hardly believe that the family were all together again. She unpacked her suitcase. Her few things easily fitted into two drawers, leaving two more for Tim who sleepily rolled out of the lower bunk wondering where he was. Lucy hung up her Brownie tunic and put on her swimsuit as her mother came in carrying hers.

"Which day do I go to Brownies?" Lucy asked.

"Oh dear, oh dear," Mum sighed.

"Oh-dear-oh-dear what?"

"You see, Dad and I are still trying to find out whether you can be a Brownie here. There used to be a Pack in the school, but so far we haven't been able to find another one. The townships — that's the villages — are all so far apart."

Lucy's mouth dropped open and she wondered how she was going to manage not to cry. She could live without her doll's house and without Granny — because she was coming to stay later — but to have to live without Brownies seemed almost impossible.

"But Mummy, I've specially cut off my sleeves," was all Lucy could say.

"What about Cubs?" asked Tim.

"No Cub Scouts either."

"Never mind. I'll wait till I'm old enough to be a Scout."

"It's all right for you," Lucy said. "You've never been a Cub. But I'm a Brownie already and I *need* to find a Pack."

They set off for the swimming pool, which was down a path past the classrooms where they would start work next day. It was a big pool, already half full of happy splashing African children. Two older students came out of the water to help Tim and Lucy down into the shallow end. One held Tim up while he tried to swim, and another stood by as Lucy swam her first width. By the time Mum had joined them she had done a length too, and was practising diving underwater for the tin plate she had brought. It was lovely and cool in the water, but Lucy kept thinking what a waste it was to learn these particular things if she never had a chance to be tested.

She felt the same when they went back to their new home. Before she had left England she had been nearly ready for taking House Orderly Badge.

"But what's the point of cleaning out an empty cupboard and washing the shelves if I can't ever do the badge?" she said to Tim.

"Aren't Brownies supposed to be helpful, specially at home?" Tim said.

"I would be helpful anyway, but we weren't allowed to bring enough of our things to put on the shelves, so there's no point in keeping on washing them."

"Don't you have a thing called a Brownie smile?"

"All right then," Lucy said crossly, and gave him a forced grin. But as soon as her mouth started to turn up at the corners, even in a comical grin, her crossness disappeared and she felt almost happy again. The smile, however funny, seemed to make Tim look happier, too.

School went well next day. The other children were friendly and welcoming, and Lucy did quite well in the lessons that were taught in English, but very badly in the lessons that were taught in the local language of Shona. But the African teacher did not mind a bit, and just laughed at Lucy's mistakes, so Lucy laughed too, and so did the children nearest her. This way they made friends and asked Lucy to join their games in the playground. Mostly they were easy games of running and catching, and follow-my-leader, with lots of shouting and singing and jokes.

After a week there was still no news of a Brownie Pack. Their parents had asked the other teachers and everyone they met to try to find out about Brownies.

Then, one hot afternoon after school, something very exciting happened. Lucy and Tim had had their rest and Tim was playing football with some other boys, barefooted because it was too hot for boots or shoes. Lucy was wandering about in the tall grass, missing her doll's house almost as much as her Brownie Pack, when she saw an African girl running along the path that went past the swimming pool. The girl was clearly wearing the Brownie uniform that Lucy had seen in a painting book before she left England! Lucy decided to follow her. She was quite a fast runner, but not fast enough! The path curved out of sight and the Brownie disappeared with it.

Lucy turned back and walked home. Mum was getting tea ready.

"There must be Brownies," Lucy said, "because I've seen one!"

"You have? Where? What's she like?"

"I don't know!" Lucy replied. "She ran too fast for me to see her face!"

When Lucy went to sleep that night she was sure she would find out all about it in school next day.

As the other children arrived Lucy looked carefully at each girl to see if she might be the one she had seen running in Brownie uniform. She was still too shy to ask each one separately, "Are you the Brownie I saw yesterday?" and *much* too shy to shout the question out loud for all to hear: "Is anyone here a Brownie?"

After school Mum said she would ask Lucy's teacher to ask the class.

"Oh no, Mummy, please don't. I don't mind being laughed at over school work. We all laugh together over that. But I wouldn't want to look silly because I don't know which girl I saw yesterday."

"No, I suppose not."

"Well, you saw the Brownie on Monday," said Tim, "so we know Monday's her Brownie day. We'd both better be on the look-out in the same place next Monday. I don't mind missing a bit of football."

"D'you think it would be all right if I put my uniform on so that whoever she is, she'll notice and stop to tell me where she's going?" Lucy suggested.

"Good idea," said Tim. So that is what they did on the next Monday afternoon.

They were down by the path well before the time Lucy had seen the Brownie the week before.

"We'll lie in wait and ambush her," said Tim as they settled down on the far side of a low bush, "only I wish she were an elephant!"

But this time, although the Brownie was not running as fast as last week, she moved so quietly that Lucy and Tim did not hear her or see her until she was well past their bush, and they were too well hidden for her to see them. They jumped up and ran after her.

"Hi! Hi! Stop!" Tim shouted. "Stop, Brownie, stop!" But she did not turn her head. "You call her," Tim said. "Maybe she doesn't listen to boys."

But she did not stop for Lucy either and then they knew why. Round the corner the school bus which had brought them from the airport was backing into a siding, and its rattling and roaring had drowned their voices. The back door opened and the Brownie popped up into the back and the bus lumbered off down the winding track they had come up when they arrived.

"Quick, Lucy! Come on!" Tim dragged her along by her wrist. "The track winds round again just below where the bus started. If we take a short cut we can get down there before the bus comes round the long way. It's my teacher driving it, I think." Before she had time to think, Lucy was scrambling down the rocky bank with Tim. They reached the side of the track just as the bus came bumping round the corner. The teacher stopped.

"Another Brownie?" he called out. "Jump in quickly then." Tim gave Lucy a push as the door opened again at the back and a hand reached down and pulled her up into the shadowy darkness.

"Don't worry," Tim called after her. "I'll tell Mum where you're going."

But where was she going? She had no idea. Now that she was getting so near to finding a Brownie Pack, wherever it might be, she was not so sure that she wanted to. She had just put on her uniform so that the other Brownie would see she was one too, and tell her about the Pack. She might have started to cry if the Brownie had not moved over from her side of the landrover to sit beside her.

"Hello, Lucy," the other Brownie greeted her. "I didn't know you were a Brownie too. Are you joining the Pack I'm in?"

"I don't know," said Lucy. "I mean, I don't know where it is. And the Pack doesn't know I want to."

"It's in the township where I used to live until my father came to teach at our school," the other Brownie said.

"Perhaps they won't want another Brownie," said Lucy. "I didn't really mean to come."

"Of course the Pack will want you," the Brownie said. "And when I tell them we are in the same class at school Wise Bird will want to put you in the same Six as mine. She'll say Nyarai is a Pixie so her friend shall be a Pixie too."

Lucy smiled happily as she realised the Brownie was in her class. "I wonder why my Mum didn't find out you were a Brownie as your Dad's a teacher too?" she said. "She promised to ask all the other teachers if they knew about a Pack."

"That's easy," said Nyarai. "My Dad's been in hospital since you came. He's only just come home."

They started to compare uniforms and Lucy told Nyarai how she had made two hand puppets after she had shortened her sleeves. "But I haven't got a shoulder sash like you have to sew my badges on," she said.

"Sister Bird will have a sash for you," Nyarai said.

"We call our Wise Bird 'Brown Owl'," Lucy said, "and we call our Sister Bird 'Tawny'." They chatted away together until the bus stopped and everybody climbed out. Under a big tree covered in fiery blossom several other Brownies were sitting and standing, or swinging on the branches. Some of the Brownies were African and some were white. Wise Bird was African and Sister Bird was white.

"Hello, Lucy," Wise Bird greeted her. "I'm so glad you have come today. I was going to send a message with Nyarai to ask you to come along with her next week."

Lucy shook hands with her left hand and wondered how Wise Bird knew her name before Nyarai had had time to tell her.

"We had a letter from your Brownie Guider in England," Sister Bird explained. "She wrote to our Commissioner asking which Pack was nearest to your school so that you could be transferred to it."

"Please can Lucy be in the Pixies?" Nyarai asked. "As she's my school friend?" Lucy felt very proud to be Nyarai's friend. Nyarai was a Second in the Pixie Six and one day would be a Sixer.

The Pack Meeting started with dancing round in a Brownie Ring just the same as at home, for subscriptions and Pack notices. Then, after some games, they all gathered round in a Pow-Wow to talk about important Brownie matters and this was when Wise Owl asked Lucy to tell them something about her Pack at home. "What is your Motto?"

"Lend a Hand."

"So is ours! Ours is Lend a Hand, too!" The Brownies all talked at once. "And the Promise is almost the same! And the Law means the same!"

Lucy went home on the bus feeling so happy she could hardly stop smiling. Now she had found a Brownie Pack for every week and a Brownie friend for every day.

She and Nyarai were almost exactly the same age.

Both their fathers were teachers at the same school. Both had brothers who were in the same class, and both loved swimming and were nearly ready to take Swimmer Badge!

Back by the school swimming pool the next day they compared notes about the test, which is harder in Zimbabwe because the weather is so good that Brownies can swim all year round. They have to be able to swim further and stay afloat longer.

Tim came strolling by wih Nyarai's brother.

"You're not the only ones with a Pack," said Tim. "We're having one too — a Cub Scout Pack and it's going to start right here in the school on February 22nd."

Lucy and Nyarai looked at each other and gave a real Brownie smile.

"February 22nd is Thinking Day!" they both said together.

"Thinking what?" Tim asked.

"Thinking about all the Brownies and Cubs and Scouts and Guides all over the world," Lucy said. "It's the birthday of the man who invented them all."

"And his wife, too," said Nyarai. "She was the World Chief Guide."

"They can't both have had their birthdays on the same day," Tim said.

"Well, they did," said Lucy.

"So the very day you and my brother start being Cub Scouts," added Nyarai, "Lucy and I will be going to special Thinking Day Revels with many other Brownie Packs."

"You know, Nyarai, as well as Swimmer Badge, I think we should do Brownie Friendship Badge," said Lucy.

"Yes, we can find out about the Brownie uniforms and badges and flags of many other countries," Nyarai said. "And teach each other games from our own countries."

"And then," said Lucy, "we'll be being real Brownie Friends!"

# HAPPY BIRTHDAY TO US!

I expect by now you know that 1984 is a very special year for Brownie Guides. We will be 70 years old!

Long ago, in 1914, there were no Brownies, only Guides. Those girls who were not yet eleven were very envious of their elder sisters and used to tag along to the meetings, watching everything the Guides did. They longed to join in but were too young.

Eventually, some wise person decided something should be done for all these would-be-Guides, and so groups were started up for younger girls. They were named Rosebuds, not a very suitable title for such adventurous young people! Their uniform was quite like that of the Guides, in dark blue, and sometimes they wore large sailor hats and carried white haversacks.

The Rosebuds were led by Guide Patrol Leaders and worked very closely with the Guide Company. They did testwork, and learnt useful knots and how to fly the Union flag. Agnes Baden-Powell, the sister of Lord Baden-Powell, designed the badge the Rosebuds wore.

The Rosebuds loved everything about being Rosebuds except their name! And in 1915 it was finally changed to Brownies, much more suitable for such industrious people! The Brownie Constitution was drawn up in December of that year and Brownies were really on their way!

In the new constitution six or eight Brownies would form a Patrol and would be led by a Guide. They didn't have Sixes and Sixers yet, you see. The uniform was to be brown now, but those Brownies who had blue uniforms were still allowed to wear them. The Company Leader was called Brown Owl, and the story of Tommy and Betty and the Wise Old Owl was adopted as inspiration for much of the Brownies' programme — I expect you know the story well.

In the early days, Brownie groups were quite large. Many had 30 or 40 Brownies and some had as many as 90! Can you imagine the poor Brown Owl trying to organise them? Later on the Patrols became Sixes, but for quite a few years, the leaders of the Sixes were still Guides.

Is your Pack doing anything special to celebrate the 70th birthday? Perhaps you will be having a 70th birthday party!

This is the earliest Brownie uniform, introduced in 1915.

# SCREEN DREAMS

## Photographs courtesy of the Children's Film and Television Foundation

Do you like watching films at the cinema or on television? Have you ever thought what it would be like to star in a film? The Children's Film and Television Foundation makes films for children, starring children. I went to see one of their most recent films and then interviewed one of the 'stars'.

The film was called **FRIEND OR FOE** and is about two boys, David and Tucky, who are evacuated from London during the second world war. They are sent to stay with a farmer and his wife in the country, and one day they find two German airmen whose plane has been shot down. The film is very exciting and I enjoyed it very much.

A few days later I went to meet John Holmes, who plays the part of David.

John was eleven when the film was made. He is a pupil at the local comprehensive school, but two evenings a week he goes to Anna Scher's Children's Theatre in north London. The director of **FRIEND OR FOE**, John Krish, went along to Anna Scher's and several of the boys auditioned for the parts of David and Tucky. John didn't know much about the film at that time, just that the actors chosen had to like animals and be able to swim!

Once the two boys had been chosen, they were given copies of the script to study.

John finds it fairly easy to learn lines, particularly for a film, when you can always have a quick look at the script before a scene is shot. He had recently been in the play **A Midsummer Night's Dream**, at school, and found this more difficult, as you must be word-perfect for a play, and have to know the whole thing before the performance.

The film was shot during the summer holidays so the children didn't miss any school. For seven days they rehearsed in a studio, then started to film. As the film location was Beaconsfield, which is not far from London, John, and Mark Luxford who played Tucky, travelled out there each day. It took five weeks to film, and John said on the last day they had a party to celebrate!

The film is set in 1940 so John had to wear old-fashioned clothes. He didn't mind this but he did mind having to wear a lot of make up! The two boys had to look very pale at the beginning of the film when they arrive in the country from the city. They also had to have their hair greased down!

Keith Chegwin starred in the title role of ROBIN HOOD JUNIOR

the kitten was now called, prowled around us, obviously feeling that he was a film star too, and should be interviewed!

John's favourite actor is Dennis Waterman, who stars in the television series **MINDER**. I told John that Dennis Waterman had started his acting career working for the Children's Film Foundation when he was quite young. The Foundation has been making films for over thirty years, originally to be shown to children at Saturday morning picture shows but, in 1982, it became The Children's Film and Television Foundation and many of the films will now be on television. Quite a number of film and television stars started their careers working on films for the Foundation, among them Frazer Hines, Keith Chegwin, Susan George, Richard O'Sullivan and Michael Crawford. Perhaps one day the name John Holmes will be as familiar to us as these.

Frazer Hines was very young in PERIL FOR THE GUY

Once they had begun work on the film, John discovered why he had been asked at the audition whether he could swim. In the story, David falls into the river and nearly drowns. John had to do this and found it quite difficult as he's not a particularly good swimmer. He is rescued by one of the German airmen, and this faces David and Tucky with a problem. The German has saved David's life, but because of the war, they should report him. I hope you will get the chance to see the film so you can find out what David and Tucky do in the end.

The other requirement of the actors was that they like animals. This was because the film was set on a farm, although the actual house used in the film was not a farmhouse. Animals were 'borrowed' from a neighbouring farm, when they were needed. If you see the film you may notice that John is often seen carrying a kitten. A cat from the neighbouring farm had produced young, and John grew fond of this particular kitten. The director decided to leave the shots of the kitten in the film. When the filming finished John was allowed to keep the kitten. As I interviewed him, Tiddles, as

BLOW YOUR OWN TRUMPET starred Michael Crawford as a young musician

# PUZZLE PAGE

by Suzanne Brown

## Word puzzle

1. One of the Brownie Journeys
2. A small group of Brownies
3. (across) An . . . . . is on the Pathfinder Badge
3. (down) There is an . . . on the Toymaker Badge
4. February 22nd is . . . . . . . . Day
5. A Brownie Six
6. Special Brownie parties
7. A Brownie who makes things can work for her . . . . . Badge
8. One of the Brownie Journeys
9. A Brownie Six
10. The . . . . . Leprechauns are a Brownie Six
11. Laid out-of-doors for Brownies to follow

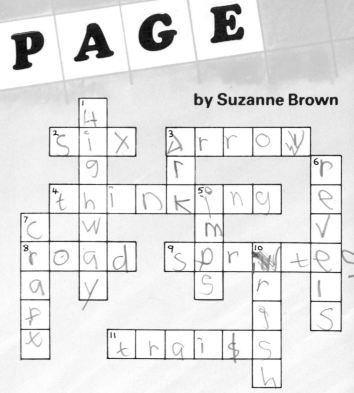

◀ **Crossword**

## Across

1. Special matters are discussed in . . . . . .
6. Used in gardening
7. There is a saucepan on this badge
8. A Brownie Six
10. The Needleworker Badge involves . . . ing
12. " . . . . a hand" is the Brownie Guide Motto
14. A Brownie promises to do her best "to . . . . . the Queen"
15. Used in carpentry
16. Working for this badge includes growing plants

## Down

1. Groups of Brownies
2. Making things out of wood
3. Necessary for the Knitter Badge
4. There is a horse . . . . on the Pony Rider Badge
5. Found on the Craft Badge
9. A Good Turn may become a Brownie . . . . . . .
11. May be grown indoors
12. A Brownie who likes bal . . . may work for her Dancer Badge
13. "I promise that I will . . my best"
14. A Brownie may do this for her Jester Badge

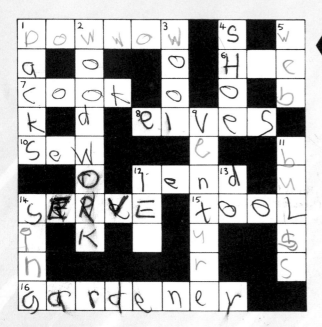

## Word puzzle

1. Listed in a recipe
2. A Brownie Six
3. Some Packs have one of these in the middle of their Ring
4. A . . . . . . . . is used for finding directions
5. A small group of Guides
6. . . . . path is the first Brownie Journey
7. A Brownie might keep stamps, shells, or postcards for her . . . . . . . . . . Badge
8. (across) Knowledge of the Highway Code is important if you are working for this badge
8. (down) There is a . . . on the Hostess Badge
9. Emergency distress signal (abbreviation)
10. A Brownie promises to do her best "to . . . . other people"
11. " . . . . . me and turn me and show me the elf"

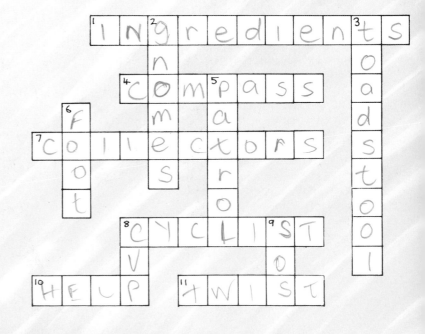

*Solutions on page 61*

# NATURE QUIZ

Bumble bee

1. What sort of bee is this?
2. What sort of shell is this?

3. What is another name for a viper?
4. Snails can have as many as 25,000 teeth. True or false?
5. What sort of tree is this?

6. Which elephant has the largest ears, African or Indian?
7. How many different species of butterfly do you think there are in the British Isles? 28, 46 or 69?
8. Where did the golden hamster originally come from?
9. A fly can beat its wings 1,000 times a second. True or false?

10. What tree do these come from?
11. How many different moths do you think there are in the British Isles? 500, 900 or 2,000?
12. Which is the largest creature that has lived on the earth or in the sea?
13. Centipedes are vegetarian. True or false?
14. How many legs does a spider have?
15. Shrimps are larger than prawns. True or false?

Solutions on page 61.

# Cook for a day!

## by Doreen Forni

Imagine that your Mum or Dad have asked you to look after the meals for a whole day. Perhaps they are busy decorating, or gardening, or maybe you have decided to take over in the kitchen as a birthday treat. Of course, you will have to have a little help lighting the oven and handling hot dishes and, if you are not very tall, when you're using the top of the cooker, but if you follow the instructions you should be able to do most of the cooking yourself. You have probably used scales in your maths lessons at school and you may even have done some cooking already, but if you are not sure about anything, do ask an adult.

Here is the menu for the day:

*Breakfast*
**Cereal**
**Boiled eggs and toast**
**Tea or coffee**
*Lunch*
**Crusty tuna pie**
**Baked apples**
*Tea*
**Scones**
**Sausage Rolls**
**Chocolate crumb cake**

Illustrated by Ivan Ripley

You will have to make a list of the ingredients you need and make sure that you have them all before you begin.

Before you begin, wash your hands and tie your hair back. Put on an apron and you're ready to start.

## BREAKFAST

To boil eggs, half fill a small saucepan with cold water and put it on the cooker. Switch on the gas or electricity high until the water boils.

Carefully take the pan off the heat and lower the eggs into the water using a tablespoon or a large spoon with holes.

Put the pan back on the ring, and as soon as the water begins to boil again turn the heat down so that the water is just gently bubbling.

If you have an egg timer set it now, or check your watch. For a boiled egg with set white and a runny yolk it should cook for 3½-4 minutes.

Make the toast now, and don't forget to keep an eye on it.

When the eggs are ready, switch off the heat, and carefully remove them from the water with a large spoon.

Put them into egg cups and serve them with toast cut into fingers.

# LUNCH

You need to begin preparing the lunch one hour before you want to serve it.

## Crusty Tuna Pie

You will need:
1 large tin tuna
1 tin condensed mushroom soup
2 packets plain crisps
2 slices bread, brown or white
50g/2oz Cheddar or Cheshire cheese

1 Light the oven at gas mark 4/180°C/350°F.
2 Open the tin of tuna and drain off the oil, holding the tuna in with the lid. Put the tuna into a basin.
3 Open the soup and add it to the tuna, then mix the two together with a fork. Add a pinch of salt and a shake of pepper.
4 Grease a 1-pint ovenproof pie dish with a margarine or butter paper, then put the tuna mixture in the bottom of the dish.
5 Using a rolling pin, crush the crisps while they are still in the bags, then put the crushed crisps into a clean bowl.
6 Grate the cheese, then grate the bread into breadcrumbs, and mix them both with the crisps.
7 Put the crispy mixture on top of the tuna and neaten it with a fork.
8 Put the dish on a baking tray and put it in the centre of the oven for 30 minutes until it is crispy and golden on top.

You can serve this on its own or with a salad.

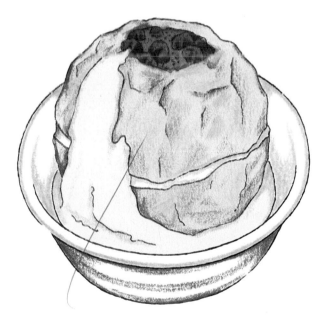

## Baked Apples

You will need:
1 cooking apple per person
25g/1oz brown sugar per apple
25g/1oz sultanas per apple

1 Light the oven at gas mark 4/180°C/350°F. If you are making the Crusty Tuna Pie your oven should already be lit at this temperature.
2 Make a hole through the centre of each apple using an apple corer or a potato peeler, to remove the core. Then make a cut round the middle of each apple, just cutting through the skin.
3 Put the apples into an ovenproof pie dish and then fill the holes in them with a mixture of the sugar and sultanas, pressing it well in.
4 Pour a little water into the dish around the apples (about 1cm deep).
5 Put the dish on a baking tray and put into the oven on the bottom shelf.
6 Cook apples for 30-40 minutes until they feel soft when you push a skewer into them.

Serve them hot or cold, with custard or icecream.

## TEA

You can prepare the tea any time during the afternoon, as the scones and sausage rolls can be eaten hot or cold.

## Sausage Rolls

You will need:
225g/8oz sausage meat or pork sausages
100g/4oz packet frozen puff pastry, defrosted

1 Light the oven at gas mark 6/200°C/400°F.
2 Lightly grease a baking tray.
3 If you are using sausages, remove the skins, cutting them off with scissors. Flour your work surface and your hands.
4 Divide the sausage meat in two, and roll each half into a long sausage shape with your hands. The 'sausage' should be about 12" long. Then clean the board.
5 Roll out the pastry carefully, keeping it in a rect-angle until it is about 30 cm/12" x 25cm/10" in size.
6 Put one long 'sausage' on the pastry as in the dia gram. Damp the top edge of the pastry with water, then fold it over the sausage meat. Press the pastry to-gether firmly.
7 With a knife cut along the pastry edge that you have pressed together. Then cut the long roll into eight smaller sausage rolls, and put them on the baking tray.
8 Repeat this with the rest of the sausage meat and the piece of pastry you have left.
9 When all the rolls are on the baking tray, brush them with a little milk, then put them in the centre of the oven for 10-15 minutes, un-til they are lightly brown and crisp.
10 Take them out of the oven and put them on a cooling tray, or serve them warm.

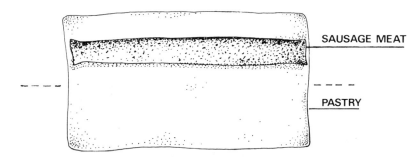

SAUSAGE MEAT

PASTRY

## Scones

You will need:
225g/8oz self-raising flour
50g/2oz block margarine or butter
1 egg
nearly 15ml/¼ pint milk
25g/1oz sugar
75–100g/3–4oz dried fruit

1 Light the oven at gas mark 6/200°C/400°F.
2 Lightly grease a baking tray.
3 Put the flour into a basin and then put in the marga-rine or butter.
4 Using a round-bladed knife cut the margarine into small pieces in the flour. When it is in fairly small pieces and coated with flour, use your fingertips to rub it in, until the mixture looks like breadcrumbs. You must do this very lightly so the mixture stays dry and white.
5 Stir in the sugar and dried fruit.
6 Break the egg into a mea-suring jug and beat it lightly with a fork, then add enough milk to make it up to 15ml/¼ pint.
7 Pour the egg and milk into the dry ingredients and stir until it is all well mixed.
8 Lightly flour your working surface and turn out the dough. Then very gently roll it out using a floured rolling pin until it is about 1.25cm/ ½" thick.
9 Using a medium-sized round pastry cutter, cut out the scones and put them on the baking tray. Gather up the bits left over, roll them out and re-cut until you have used all the dough.
10 Put the scones on the tray in the centre of the oven and bake them for 10-15 minutes until they are well-risen and golden brown.
11 When you've taken them out of the oven, put them on a cooling tray.

Serve them cut in half and buttered. Scones are best eaten the day they are made.

## Chocolate Crumb Cake

This delicious biscuit cake doesn't need any baking.
You will need:
225/8oz digestive biscuits or other plain sweet biscuits
100g/4oz block margarine or butter
1 tbsp cocoa
1 tbsp golden syrup
2 tbsp sugar
225g/8oz cooking chocolate (optional)

1 Lightly grease a swiss-roll tin using a butter paper. (If you don't have a swiss-roll tin, a cake or flan tin will do).
2 Put the biscuits into a plastic bag and crush them with a rolling pin until they are well broken up.
3 Put the margarine, cocoa, syrup and sugar into a small saucepan, and gently heat them until everything has just melted.
4 Put the broken biscuit into a bowl and pour on the melted ingredients. Stir until thoroughly mixed.
5 Spread the mixture into the greased tin and press down well.
6 Break up the cooking chocolate onto a tin plate and put the plate over a pan containing hot (not boiling) water until it has melted.
7 Pour the melted chocolate over the biscuit mixture and put the tray into the refrigerator until it has set, then cut it into squares.

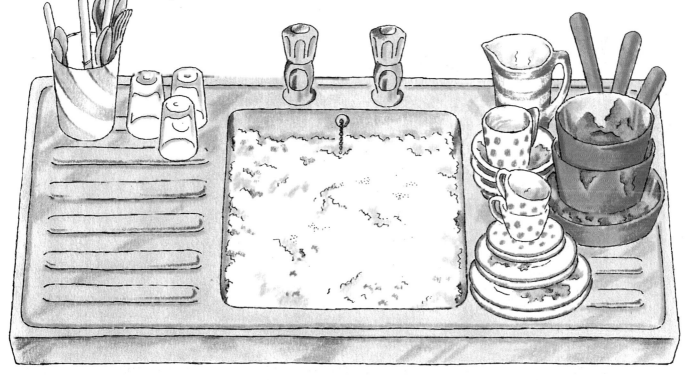

## Last but not least!

Now for the worst job! The washing-up! It's no treat for anyone if you leave the kitchen in a dreadful mess, so always clear up as you go along wherever possible. Stack all the things to be washed beside the sink, then clean down your work surfaces, and wipe the top of the cooker. Run some washing-up water as hot as you can stand it, putting in a squirt of washing-up liquid. Now you are ready to begin.

Start with any glasses, washing them carefully one at a time. Cutlery comes next, then cups, saucers, bowls and plates. Last of all you wash the very dirty and greasy pans. If necessary, change the water halfway through as you may find it getting scummy.

Empty the washing-up bowl and rinse it and the sink. Dry all the cutlery and crockery and put it away, then hang the tea-towel to dry. The kitchen should now look as tidy as when you started.

# HONEY BEES

**Worker bee foraging for nectar in borage.**

photographs by Norman Redfern

Since ancient times people valued bees for the honey produced by wild bee colonies in hollow trees and logs. Later they realised it was more convenient to keep the bees in portable containers, such as straw skeps, wicker baskets and earthenware pots. Bee hives like the ones we see today were not used before the nineteenth century.

Healing with honey is mentioned in the Bible, the Talmud and the Koran. It was even used as a beauty treatment by the Queen of Sheba and Cleopatra. In the Middle Ages honey was put on wounds, burns, ulcers and infections and taken as a remedy for coughs and colds, just as today we may make a honey and lemon drink when we feel a cold coming on.

The Romans, Greeks and Egyptians all drank mead, an alcoholic liquor of fermented honey and water.

Under Roman law, swarming bees were classified as wild creatures and anyone who caught them could keep them. Because of this the ritual of 'tanging' arose. The beekeeper would run after the swarm, loudly banging on a kettle or pan to let the neighbourhood know that the swarm in the air belonged to him.

A traditional way to get bees to settle was to throw a shower of fine earth over them so they would think it was starting to rain and quickly alight somewhere to shelter, or, if you were lucky, rush back to the hive. Bees prefer fine weather. If it's wet or thundery they stay inside the hive. Damp and windy weather makes them bad tempered. As the saying goes:

If the bees stay at home,
Rain will soon come.
If they fly away,
Fine will be the day.

Bees that swarm in May have time to set up a new colony and produce plenty of honey before the summer is over, but by July there is not enough time for the bees to gather enough nectar before the autumn (in fact the beekeeper must be careful to leave enough honey in the hive to feed the bees through the winter).

A swarm of bees in May
Is worth a load of hay.
A swarm of bees in June
Is worth a silver spoon.
A swarm of bees in July
Is scarcely worth a fly.

Here are a few legends and superstitions concerning bees and honey.

If you wish your bees to thrive
Gold must be paid for every hive,
For when they're bought with other money
There will be neither swarm nor honey.

For anyone without gold coin, it was better to exchange the bees for goods, a piglet or some corn. To give away a hive was very bad luck.

Bees and honey were thought to have special properties. According to Greek mythology, the gift of eloquent speech was conferred on all whose lips were touched by bees. They were believed to be wise, so people confided their secrets to them, along with any important events in the family such as births, marriages and deaths. This was known as 'telling the bees'.

Seeing a swarm of bees on one's wedding day was a good omen and if a bee went to the wedding on the bride's bouquet this was especially lucky. The bride would creep out to the hive early in the day and whisper:

"Little brownies, little brownies,
Your mistress is to be wed."

To make doubly sure of the bees' blessing, the bride would leave a piece of wedding cake outside the hive.

The hive was seen as a model of industry and harmony in the home. Bees would not thrive in a quarrelsome family and wouldn't tolerate arrogance, impatience or immorality. Conversely, if a hive became lazy, disaster would be sure to follow.

I was lucky enough to visit some bee hives belonging to Michael Coward who is the Secretary of the British Beekeepers Association. Mr Coward has four hives situated at the end of his garden. As we walked up to them Mr Coward said how lucky we were that the weather was fine, as the bees should be in a good mood. I was relieved to hear this!

Before we left the house, we had both put protective veils over our heads, and Mr Coward had prepared the bee-smoker. This is a device like a small pair of bellows, which is used to puff smoke into the hive before it is opened. Once the bees were subdued, Mr Coward opened up the hive, and then took off his veil, as he found it easier to work without one. I was surprised that he didn't wear gloves, either, but he said most beekeepers prefer to work with bare hands. I asked him if he was ever stung.

"Oh yes, quite often!" he replied, but it didn't hurt much, as like most beekeepers he has built up an immunity to stings. Bees sting in defence, when they are frightened, so the best way to avoid being stung is to treat them gently, and not annoy them. If you are unlucky there are several ways to soothe the pain. Lemon juice, honey and iodine all help. If the sting can be seen, don't try to press it out. Instead scrape it off with a fingernail. About one person in fifty is allergic to bee stings and should be careful when there are bees about and seek medical aid if stung.

I was rather worried about being stung myself, as I had bare arms and legs, but in the end the only thing to sting me was a nettle!

This hive housed the best-tempered bees.

**Mr Coward prepares the bee-smoker and then puffs some smoke into one of the hives to calm down the bees inside.**

We looked to see if there were any cells with eggs or larvae in them in this frame.

Mr Coward explains the difference between the cells for drones and workers.

This frame is almost full of honey. When the cells are full the bees put a cap over them. Here there are just a few uncapped cells round the edges.

There are three different types of honey bees: the workers, the drones and the queen.

## Workers

A hive will have about 500,000 workers all busily collecting nectar and pollen. They also do the housework, clearing out debris from the bottom of the hive and building and repairing the honeycombs. In the summer the workers live only a few weeks, but the ones born in the autumn live through the winter.

## Drones

Drones are larger than workers and have no sting. Each hive has about two hundred and their only purpose is to fertilise the queen. At the end of the summer they are of no further use and so are starved by the workers and then turned out of the hive to die. There should be no drones in a hive in winter.

## The Queen

The queen bee is really just an egg-laying machine. She starts laying in January, a few eggs at a time, but by mid-summer she could be laying as many as two thousand eggs a day. She is fed and groomed by the workers and usually lives for two to three years.

illustrations by Phil Weare

A hive has only one queen, but sometimes the workers will start building queen-cells, which hang free rather than being part of the honeycomb. The larvae that hatch in these cells are fed on royal jelly, a special substance which enables them to develop into queen bees. After eight days these cells are capped and a week later the new queens will start to emerge. One of them will kill the others and take over the hive. A few days before this happens the old queen will leave the hive with a swarm to establish a new colony. The beekeeper has to look for any queen-cells and destroy them, to prevent the bees swarming.

During the summer the bees produce honey which they store as honeycomb in boxes called 'supers'. The bee-keeper puts the supers on top of the hive specially for this. The queen is excluded from the supers by a special grid so no eggs are laid in them.

# HONEY RECIPES

Before the eighteenth century, when sugar became widely available, honey was the principle sweetener in cookery. It was also used for curing and preserving.
There are many recipes in which you can use honey instead of sugar. Honey bread, honey cakes, honey biscuits, honey pudding and honey sauce are all delicious.

## Honeyade

Boil together about 6 tbsp chopped mint, a teacup of honey, a teacup of water and 2 tbsp lemon juice.
Simmer this gently for about 10 minutes, then strain and leave to cool.
Diluted with water, this makes a most refreshing drink.

## Honey Chicken

4 chicken pieces, skinned
1 egg
30ml/2tbsp cooking oil
30ml/2tbsp soy sauce
30ml/2tbsp lemon juice
15ml/1tbsp paprika
50g/2oz honey
5g/1tsp salt

Light the oven at 180°C/350°F/gas mark 4.
Arrange the chicken pieces on a buttered ovenproof dish.
Beat together all the other ingredients in a bowl, then spoon the mixture over the chicken.
Put the dish in the oven and bake for 1 hour, turning and basting the chicken pieces frequently.
For the last 10 minutes, turn the oven up slightly to crisp the outside.

## Honey Biscuits

350g/12oz plain flour
15g/½oz baking powder
1 tsp mixed spice
100g/4oz caster sugar
350g/12oz honey
50g/2oz mixed peel
1 egg

Light the oven at 190°C/375°F/gas mark 5.
Sift the flour, baking powder and mixed spice into a bowl, then stir in the sugar.
In a small pan, melt the butter and honey, then pour them into the flour and stir them in. Add the mixed peel.
Beat the egg in a cup, then add that to the mixture, combining it together to form a dough.
Flour your work surface, then roll out the dough until it is about 1.5cm/½"thick.
Using a round pastry cutter, cut out biscuits and put them on a lightly greased baking tray.
Put them in the oven and cook for about 15 minutes.

# by Agnes Szudek
illustrated by Viv Quillin

The school at the far end of the town looked like a centre of very serious learning. It was neat, and sedate, with stout walls of golden iron-stone and long windows like high arched eyebrows. A notice beside the iron gate gave a brief piece of information:

Bordering the small neatly-cropped school grounds were the spacious fields of Potter's Farm, and beyond them the open countryside.

As my story begins, it was November the fifth and time for school dinner. A line of hungry children waited to file into the dinner-hall. Today, Miss Browbeater was supervising the meal, and she was being extra strict. With bonfire night looming, she was determined to keep the excitement down. Along the line she strode, tight-lipped, dishing out black marks like free samples.

"Florrie Nightingale, two black marks for hanging on the door-handle like that. You know you'll have it off. And Georgie Stephenson, get rid of that gum immediately. You've had your marshmallows, potato crisps and cream biscuits with milk, so what more do you need before your dinner? Besides, chewing-gum's bad for you."

As Georgie slouched off to deposit his gum, probably behind his ear, Miss Browbeater's attention was taken by a dark head bobbing up and down beside her in the queue, a head spiked with multi-coloured hair ribbons.

"Cherry Pippin! You naughty sprat. How dare you come again with all that colour on your head? You know perfectly well the school colours are —"

At that moment, the huge glaring eyes of Cherry's mother peered over Miss Browbeater's shoulder. Mrs Starletta Pippin had silently appeared and come close to the headmistress's left ear. She wore a long brightly-flowered dress and was swathed in a vast black shawl that reached to the ground. From its thick fringe there shivered and flashed scores of silver stars.

"Excuse me, Miss Browbeater," she said, in a hollow, haunting voice. "My Cherry's gym shoes. She left them behind this morning, so I brought them along." Mrs Pippin produced the gym shoes from under her shawl with a swirl and a flourish, like a magician with his best trick.

"Good, good," said Miss Browbeater. "Give her the plimmies, she's over there. And Mrs Pippin, while you're here, may I remind you that I cannot allow your daughter to wear assorted colours on her scalp. The school prospectus plainly states that uniform colours are sky and sand."

Mrs Pippin, who had tossed the shoes to her daughter, now flung her shawl wide, then wrapped it tightly around her shoulders. Her amber eyes widened until they looked like two fried eggs.

"When I stepped down from my caravan this morning, madam, the sky was red, yellow, pink and blue," she said softly, dramatically. "I always look at the sky before I tie on my Cherry's ribbons. So don't tell me about the sky." She was shaking so much with annoyance that her gold bangles and dangling earrings rang like chime-bars.

"Sky means grey," said Miss Browbeater, icily. "Take your pick of light, medium, dark, clerical or elephant. So long as it's a good sky grey, that's what counts. And sand — is sand, the seaside sort."

Mrs Starletta Pippin's eyes narrowed to piercing slits as sharp as skewers, but Miss Browbeater ignored the menacing look and went on, "And what is more, if your daughter came to school in proper colours, her arithmetic might improve. It's little short of disgraceful. And of course, she wouldn't look as if she had a head full of — of — squibs! Yes, squibs!" This was the first colourful word to come into her mind on bonfire day.

...Miss Browbeater ignored the menacing look and went on.....

Mrs Pippin's breathing grew loud and heavy. "Squibs, is it? Fireworks, eh? So be it, Miss Browbeater," she said thinly, with a hissing whisper. Then she was gone, almost in a flash, leaving Miss Browbeater staring at an empty space.

Now Cherry Pippin had often said that her mother had strong gipsy powers. At first no one had believed her, although surprising and odd things had happened now and again, like the time a fourth year bully had pulled her hair till she cried. The next day two of his front teeth fell out without any warning. Fine white second teeth, they were. The children often wondered about Cherry's mother, but no one had ever visited the brightly-painted caravan at the edge of the wood, where mother and daughter lived.

In the meantime, the long dinner queue had become restless. The children shuffled into the hall, muttering about their hunger pangs. Miss Browbeater had just raised her hands to clap for silence, when an unexpected gust of wind blew the main doors wide open. It whooshed round the hall like a cyclone taking a short-cut, then whooshed out.

When the dust had settled, there on the threshold were the school dinners. But the shiny hot containers were not carried in by the usual men, Frank and Wilf. Two strangers crossed the hall in a jumble of worn-out clothes, battered hats, wellingtons, and with what looked like straw sticking out of their cuffs. But the children seemed unaware of anything odd, and greeted the strangers eagerly, waving their knives and forks.

...Two strangers crossed the hall...

"What's up for grabs? Tell us the worst."

"Bangers!" was the reply. "What else on bonfire night?"

Bangers and mash with baked beans was one of the favourite dinners, although Miss Browbeater would not allow any slang words if she heard them. She called out in top C, the note she liked to reach in emergencies.

"We are having sausages in my Academy, if you please." She stamped her foot and rattled two spoons together, but no one listened.

As the odd-looking dinner men hurried out, Miss Browbeater's gaze followed them to their van. She stared hard at the vehicle, which she did not recognise. On the side was printed:

..."The Education Office said nothing about a new dinner service"...

"Strange," she murmured. "The Education Office said nothing about a new dinner service. Industrial dispute, I expect."

But she had no time to think about it further, because the hall was in uproar.

Hurrying over to Mrs Squosh, the fiercest and most senior dinner lady, Miss Browbeater snatched the sausage tongs from her and beat them on the metal tin for silence. When at last she thought she had got it, she took a pin from her lapel, dropped it to the floor, put her hand to her ear, and was satisfied.

Turning to Mrs Squosh, she said, "Perhaps they will learn it from you, Mrs S, if they want any dinner at all. Pray, tell us, what do we have for dinner today?"

Mrs Squosh grabbed the tongs back again. She expertly flipped the lid off the tin, opened her mouth like a cellar door, and gasped, "We have — er, we have — er — er."

"Yes, dear Mrs Squosh? Yes?" urged Miss Browbeater, trying to be patient.

"It's — oh, it's — it's bangers!" shrieked Mrs Squosh with an unearthly howl. "It's bangers all right Miss, bangers!"

"How dare you!" began Miss Browbeater, but she got no further. From the oblong dinner tin came a volley of fireworks, like rockets from a firing range. Out they came, sizzling and spurting, bangers every one.

They looked like sausages, but they did not behave like sausages. Up they shot in high curving arcs round the hall, sending off showers of coloured sparks that fizzled out somewhere above the P.E. bars.

At first, the dinner ladies fell to the floor and hid their faces. But when the second tin burst open, they stumbled to their feet and ran squealing out of the hall, and out through the school gate, clutching their white caps to their heads.

They ran wildly to the banks of the river, ready to dive in at the slightest sign of pursuit, but the bangers were much too busy in the school hall.

Miss Browbeater ducked about with eyes rolling in disbelief at the greasy flying objects that were narrowly missing her head.

..They looked like sausages, but they did not behave like sausages...

"Call them off! Call them off!" she screeched, well above top C. "Two hundred black marks to everyone in this hall. Two thousand to the culprit responsible for this outrage!"

In her frenzy she gave black marks to the bangers and withdrew their afternoon play. The children roared with laughter and cheered the sausages on their way until the last one had zoomed upwards and spluttered into nothingness.

Suddenly all was quiet. Not a muscle moved. Miss Browbeater was speechless with exhaustion. Her grey hair stood up in five little tufts as it always did when things were getting the better of her.

Just then, heavy footsteps were heard outside the door. The headmistress got ready to duck as the door flew open. But this time it was Frank and Wilf, carrying the school dinner tins just as they always did. Behind them, tearful and red-faced, trotted the dinner ladies.

"S-sorry we're l-late," puffed Frank. "Would you believe it, we got stuck in traffic by the bridge and just when we thought it was clear, along comes the police, fire-brigade, Saint John Ambulance — the whole jamboree. And all on account of your dinner ladies."

"My dinner ladies, in a jamboree?" asked Miss Browbeater, confusedly.

"Making exhibitions of themselves, they were," said Wilf. "Running along the river bank shouting about sausages. D'you think we fish them out of the river, then?"

"Oh, I think I'm going to faint," said Miss Browbeater, weakly.

"Half a minute, I haven't finished yet," said Wilf indignantly. "The police were going to run them in, but we said we'd run them in here where they belong, so here we are. Right, I've finished." Wilf said this as though he was giving permission for the fainting fit to continue. Miss Browbeater obliged.

"I-I'm going. Oh, I'm going," she sighed, flopping her arms down like a rag doll.

Frank turned and waved his cap at the children.

"Better late than never. What d'you say, eh?" he shouted.

"Hooray for school dinners," yelled the children, by now hungry enough to start on their own jumpers. "Hooray! Hooray! Hooray!"

Miss Browbeater, who had still not quite fainted, drew her hand across her forehead and slowly began to fall sideways. Wilf leapt forward and caught her just before she hit the floor.

"She's weak from hunger, I expect," he said, and fanned her wildly with a dinner plate.

Miss Browbeater was not quite 'out', and pushed the plate aside.

"It's not that," she sighed. "It's the s-s-s."

"Don't you worry, love. You'll be all right once you get a bit of dinner in you. Smashing one today, too. Bangers and mash."

..." you'll be alright once you get a bit of dinner in you"...

Before he had time to announce the pudding, Miss Browbeater had slumped from his grasp.

"Bangers — and mash," she muttered to the parquet flooring, and lay quite still.

By this time the dinner ladies had composed themselves and the meal was in full swing. Two dinner plates were brought to fan the headmistress back to consciousness, and she was propped up on a chair. She seemed to be in a bad way.

"Those — bangers — you're serving," she said to Mrs Squosh. "How did you get them down from the ceiling?"

But Mrs Squosh did not want to be reminded about the earlier incident.

"Bangers off the ceiling?" she repeated. "I suppose you mean sausages, Miss Browbeater. I never had them on the ceiling. They come in tins, like this, with gravy. D'you want yours now, then?"

But the headmistress seemed to have lost her appetite. She rose from the chair and wandered away looking distinctly smoky at the ends.

"It was never like this before that Mrs Pippin came here. There must be easier ways of earning a living."

Frank and Wilf collected up the extra dinner tins, thinking they must have left them behind the day before, and the children hungrily began to eat their bangers and mash, and apple pie and custard.

But the pupils of Miss Browbeater's Academy never looked at bangers and mash in quite the same way again, and neither did Miss Browbeater. She seemed particularly uneasy each time she saw Mrs Starletta Pippin. Cherry Pippin went on wearing her multi-coloured hair ribbons, and strangely enough, not another word was said about them!

# PARVEEN'S GAME

## by Natalie Webber

illustrated by Kathleen Whapham

Parveen was helping the rest of the Sprites to make a big Thinking Day card when Brown Owl called them together for Pow-wow. Parveen put down her felt pen with a little sigh. She was younger than most of the other Brownies and hadn't been coming for very long. She hadn't nearly finished her bit of the card and now the others would think she was slow and useless.

"Come on, Parveen," called Brown Owl, "we've a lot to talk about this evening."

"Now," she went on, as Parveen sat down, "as you know, all the Brownies in the District are having a Thinking Day revels this year and we've been asked to choose a new game from another country and teach it to the other Packs. I'm a bit stuck for ideas and I wondered if you had any?"

For once the Brownies were all silent, while they gazed at each other and tried to look as though a brilliant idea was on the tip of their tongues. At last one of the Imps put her hand into the ring, to show that she wanted to speak.

"The trouble is," she said, "that we play lots of games in Brownies, but mostly we don't know where they come from and anyway the other Packs play some of them too."

"That's a problem, I know," agreed Brown Owl. "I think we need to look for something a bit different,

something that we *know* is played by Brownies in another country." She looked straight at Parveen.

Parveen looked hastily down at the floor. She had lived in India all her life until two months ago and had belonged to a Bulbul flock there. Now her father was working in London for two years, so she was coming to Brownies instead, but she often felt rather lonely and silly in her blue and white uniform when all the English Brownies were in their brown dresses. Nearly every day she longed to be back in her own dusty hot country, with her own friends. Brown Owl knew she felt shy and tried to help her.

"Think of your school in India," she said. "Did you ever play games at playtime?"

Parveen thought of her school in Bombay, a tall ugly building with tiny classrooms, built in the middle of a huge dusty playground. And she remembered sitting on the dry earth with her friends at lunchtime, eating their packed lunches from the tin boxes they always carried. And then after lunch . . .

"I can think of *one*," she said slowly, "but you need two sticks to play it."

"That's all right," said Joanna, the Sprites Sixer, "I could bring those. What do you have to do?"

"Well, first you scratch a hole in the ground and lay the short stick across it."

There was immediate uproar.

"But what if we have to be indoors?"

"Can you imagine what the caretaker will say if we carve a great hole in the floorboards?"

"That's useless, Brown Owl!"

Parveen looked miserable and Joanna came to her rescue.

"I'm sure we'll think of something. We could always prop the stick on two little blocks of wood."

"Or even on two rubbers," agreed Brown Owl. "Look, Parveen, why don't you and Pack Leader go into a corner away from this noisy lot, and write down the instructions for your game and then we'll all try playing it."

This is what Parveen wrote:

## Gillie Dander

**What you need:**

One long stick with a fairly pointed end (about as long as a cricket bat)

One much shorter stick, about 12 cms long.

**What you do:**

1. Divide the players into batters and fielders. The fielders spread out and all the batters except one sit down.

2. The batter scratches a short channel in the ground and then lays the short stick (dander) across it. If you are playing indoors, lie the short stick across two blocks of wood.

Now the batter hooks the long stick (gillie) under the dander and flicks the dander up into the air and as far as possible.

3. If one of the fielders catches it the batter is out.

4. If it falls to the ground, the fielders have another chance to get her out. She has to lay her long stick on the ground and the fielder nearest to the short stick picks it up and throws it at the long stick. If she hits it, the batter is out.

5. If she's *still* not out, she has a chance to get a point for her side — at last!

She lays the short stick back on the hole and taps it hard at one end with the long stick, to make it fly up into the air. If it flies up she gets ½ a point and she then tries to get another ½ point, by hitting it again while it is still in the air.

6. If she can't do it the first time she has two more tries. Then she goes to the back of the batting queue and the next batter has a turn.

You do this until all the batters are out and then change sides.

If you *do* play it indoors, you could use something a bit softer for the dander — like a piece of balsa wood, or a rolled-up comic cut in half. And don't play near any windows!

# WORDSQUARE

### by Ann Martin

Can you find all these words in the wordsquare? They may be written horizontally, diagonally, up or down, backwards or forwards, but they are all in straight lines.

WIDE AWAKE

BROWNIE GUIDE

THE PROMISE

LORD BADEN-POWELL

ROSEBUD

BETTY

TOMMY

MRS. OWL

TOADSTOOL

POOL

SIXER

PIXIE

IMPS

LEND A HAND

POW WOW

SALUTE

PACK LEADER

QUEEN

UNIFORM

VENTURES

ROAD

| | | | | | | | | | | | | | | | |
|---|---|---|---|---|---|---|---|---|---|---|---|---|---|---|---|
| R | P | A | C | K | L | E | A | D | E | R | O | D | Z | Q | V | L |
| S | R | L | S | I | X | E | R | R | Y | M | M | O | T | U | E | O |
| I | G | O | P | A | H | A | O | Z | T | O | A | O | R | E | N | R |
| R | D | R | W | O | L | A | M | S | H | P | I | L | R | E | T | D |
| W | A | U | Y | N | D | U | R | S | E | N | D | A | H | A | N | B |
| I | S | N | T | P | I | M | T | O | P | P | P | S | A | L | Z | A |
| D | E | I | T | I | B | E | O | E | R | O | S | E | B | U | D | D |
| E | R | F | E | X | R | Z | G | P | O | W | W | O | W | Z | T | E |
| A | U | O | B | I | O | M | H | U | M | I | L | E | Z | O | Q | N |
| W | T | R | M | E | O | R | I | P | I | M | L | E | A | U | J | P |
| A | N | M | E | R | P | S | G | O | S | D | T | D | N | N | E | O |
| K | E | B | P | I | X | O | H | O | E | I | E | P | A | Z | E | W |
| E | V | E | I | M | R | W | W | Z | S | I | Z | A | Q | U | N | E |
| Z | H | T | X | P | O | L | E | N | D | A | H | A | N | D | E | L |
| T | Z | O | I | S | S | Z | L | O | O | T | S | D | A | O | T | L |

Solution on page 61

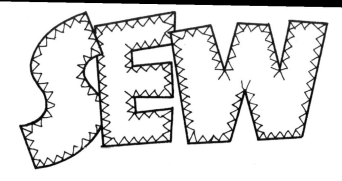

You can make one of these animals for part of your Toymaker Badge. They are made from felt and sewn using stab stitch, pushing the needle through from one side to the other.

FIRST trace the pattern, then stick the tracing onto thin card, for example old Christmas cards. Carefully cut round the shape. This is your template. Place the template onto your felt and draw round the shape, then carefully cut out the felt. When you have cut out all the pieces for one of the animals you can begin to sew. Don't make the stitches too small or they will pull through the felt when the animal is stuffed. Put the stuffing in in very small amounts, pushing it right into the legs etc of the animal.

**ELEPHANT:** To make the elephant you need one 200 mm square of grey felt, 4 pipe cleaners, grey stranded cotton for sewing.

1. Pin the two inside pieces of felt to the two main pieces, so that you have a left and right side of the animal. Sew round these leaving the straight sides free.

2. Pin the two main pieces together and sew round, starting at the tail and 'going up along the back, as far as the point marked 'gusset'.

3. Sew one side of the head to one side of the gusset, slotting in the ear at the right place. Sew to the end of the gusset, then carry on sewing round the trunk, mouth and neck, joining both sides together.

4. Sew in the other side of the gusset, putting in the other ear in the right place.

5. Very carefully stuff the head and trunk, using only a very small amount at a time, and pushing it right to the end of the trunk.

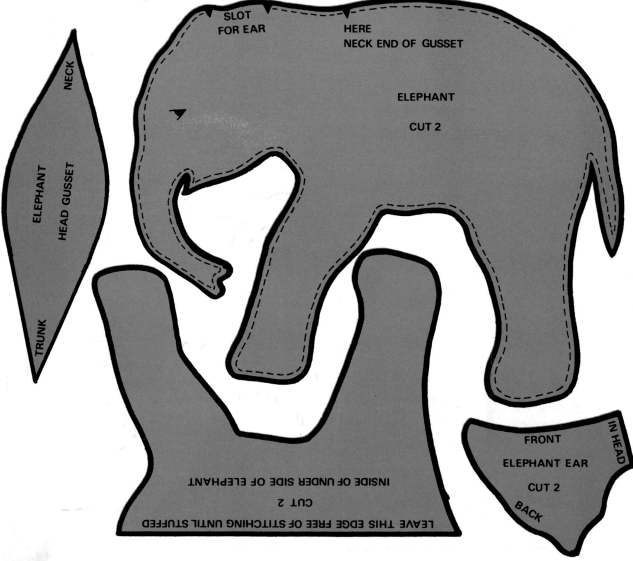

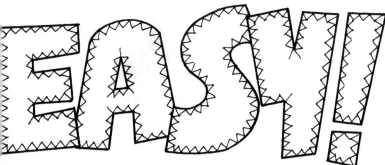

6. Bend back the ends of two of the pipe cleaners, binding them with wool or cotton to make them safe. Put one end of each cleaner in one front leg, then bend them over and put the other ends in the other front leg.

7. Now do the same with the other two pipe cleaners, binding them, then putting them in the back legs.

8. Finish stuffing the elephant, putting just a little in the legs.

9. Overlap one side of the open inside edge over the other, and sew them together, pulling the stitches quite tight.

10. Embroider a few stitches in black for the eyes.

**DOG:** To make the dog you will need one 200 mm square of brown felt, 2 pipe cleaners, brown stranded cotton for sewing. You can use anything suitable for the collar and lead such as a piece of ribbon, or a scrap of felt.

1. Pin the two inside pieces of felt to the two main pieces, making sure you have a left and a right side of the animal. Sew round these, leaving the straight inner edge free.

2. Put the two halves together and sew round the tail and along the back to the point marked 'gusset'.

3. Sew one side of the head to one side of the gusset, putting the ear piece in at the right place, sewing the head and gusset together as far as the nose.

4. Sew round the nose and under the jaw and down the neck at the front.

5. Join the other side of the head to the gusset, putting in the other ear.

6. Now stuff the head, carefully pushing the stuffing right into the nose.

7. Take the pipe cleaners and bend back the points about 35 mm at each end. Bind these with wool or cotton to make them safe.

8. Put one end of one pipe cleaner into one front leg then bend it over to make a hoop and put the other end into the other front leg.

9. Do the same for the back legs.

10. Finish stuffing the dog, then overlap one free edge of the inside body piece over the other and stitch them together, pulling these stitches quite tight.

11. Embroider a few stitches in black for the eyes.

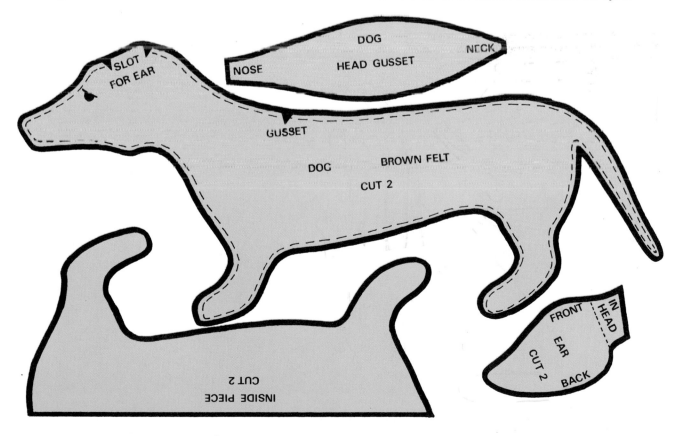

SLOT FOR EAR

NOSE    DOG HEAD GUSSET    NECK

GUSSET

DOG    BROWN FELT

CUT 2

INSIDE PIECE
CUT 2

FRONT    IN HEAD
EAR
CUT 2    BACK

# TONBRIDGE GUIDES MEET SOME GREAT DANES!

Where did you make your Promise? Probably, for most of you, it was at a Brownie meeting with the rest of the Pack around you.
But sometimes it can happen in the strangest places; recently three Ranger Guides made their Promises on a ferryboat in the middle of the North Sea!

They were members of the 17th Tonbridge Scout and Guide Band on their way to Denmark for a concert tour. The musicians were to be guests of the Allerod Spejdernes Tambourkorps, which means the Allerod Scout and Guide Band. In Denmark, Guides are called Spejders, (pronounced spiders).

The ferry crossing took twenty hours, from Harwich to Esberg, and then a coach took the band to Allerod. The Scouts and Guides

stayed with Danish band members, and as the Allerod band had visited Tonbridge the previous year, most already knew each other.

The following day, the two bands met up at Allerod school, piled into two coaches and set off for Copenhagen. After some sightseeing they went on to Rosenburg and marched through the pedestrian precinct playing for the townspeople, ending up outside the Rathaus (townhall!) where both bands put on a display.

One afternoon the bands played for some old people who had put in a special request to hear them, and another afternoon was spent beside the sea. Even the keenest swimmers were put off by the number of jellyfish however, so the next swimming session was in the

local pool!

The Guides were particularly struck by how many cyclists there were, and how almost every road had a cycle track. Denmark is very flat so it is easy to cycle everywhere.

All the Danish children spoke good English, which they learn in school from the age of eleven, and some of Tonbridge band proved to be quick at picking up Danish, although there were sometimes misunderstandings. On one occasion in a restaurant, after a trip to the fun-fair, one of the Guiders asked the waitress for the 'rutchebane', meaning the bill. Unfortunately, 'rutchebane' means big-dipper! The poor waitress didn't know what to think!

One of the highlights of the trip was a civic reception

given by the mayor of Allerod, followed by lunch in the council offices.

Another special part of the trip for many of the Scouts and Guides was the firework display in the Tivoli Gardens one evening. On the last day a party was given by the host families for all their guests and many of the Scouts and Guides swopped hats and scarves with the Spejders.

The next morning it was with sad hearts that the Tonbridge Scout and Guide Band bade their Danish friends farewell, but on the long coach journey back to Esberg a slight detour was made to visit Legoland. For some of the band members this was almost the best part of the trip, as they wandered around the miniature landscape where everything was made of Lego: houses, farms, windmills, in fact a complete Lego land!

Once on the ferry, thoughts turned to home, and all the lovely souvenirs bought for families and friends. And next year the Allerod Spejdernes Tambourkorps are coming over to Tonbridge. Perhaps they'll all swop hats and scarves back again!

# The Colours of Autumn

The autumnal equinox which occurs on or about September 21st is the moment when the sun crosses the Equator during its apparent annual motion from north to south. This is the beginning of that time of year when the foliage of some shrubs, herbs and trees looks as if an expert artist had chosen all the most glowing yellows, golds, reds, browns and purples from the paint box, and with a few skilful strokes of the brush had transformed each deciduous plant into a vision of flaming beauty.

But have you ever wondered what makes the leaves change into such lovely autumn colours? And why they fall? Or why evergreens don't appear to lose their leaves?

Well, the colouring matter in the cells and tissues of a plant, or an animal, is called pigment. The high degree of pigmentation in trees, shrubs and herbs in the autumn depends very much on the weather we have had during the summer. For instance, should

the summer be poor, and then September be warm and damp, the colours of the leaves in October and November will be dull and unexciting. A dry, dazzling summer with a moderate degree of heat, followed by a dry September with a few sharp frosts, will turn the foliage of every deciduous tree into a magnificent display of colour.

Naturally, in those countries like the United States of America and Canada, where the extremes of climate are greater than in Britain, the effect of the weather on the colours of autumn is more conspicuously illustrated. There is no more superb sight than the blazing reds and yellows of the maple trees in Canada, which a single crisp frost in September can change from a mass of green.

The work of the deciduous leaf is complete by the end of October, when it is cast off. This October leaf-shedding, though, is by no means a haphazard affair. Having acquired gorgeous autumn livery, a layer of cells at the end of the leaf stalk tear away from each other. They form a weak joint, until eventually the leaf is joined to the twig by only a single thread. The winds of autumn and winter, together with the frost, break the last link, and the leaf falls.

Perhaps you imagine that the twig would now be afflicted with an open wound of fragile living cells, liable to infection; but this is not so. The cells beneath those at the base of the leaf-stalk are yielding cork, and by the time the leaf drops off this cork has spread across the entire joint, leaving a wholesome scar, and closing off the tear so that no sap escapes. In this way, the leaves, when the tree has no further use for them as food collectors and manufacturers, are discarded.

Leaf-shedding is a living process carried out by trees to rid themselves of leaves which could cause them to lose too much moisture in the winter. You see, trees draw up water from the soil through their roots. In a temperate climate like ours, they do this mostly during the summer, because in the chill winter season they may not be able to draw up moisture from the frozen soil. So, in the winter, trees have to rely on the water they have managed to store within them. They shed their leaves to prevent any water loss through them, as plants give off water through their greenery.

Illustrated by Jennifer Northway

Some naturalists believe also that useless products are circulated through the leaves before they fall, and that this is one of the methods used by trees to rid themselves of un-needed substances.

## Evergreens

Occurring naturally in Britain are a number of evergreen trees whose leaves are especially thickened and modified to stop them losing too much water. Some, such as the laurel, have a waxy coating on the leaves, which acts as a waterproof layer to keep moisture in.

Others have very thin, needle-like leaves, which do not lose much water because of their small surface area. The elegant fir tree is one of these, and in the winter we are filled with wonder as we notice these pretty trees, which in the summer are hidden by their more colourful neighbours. It is this constancy of the evergreens that makes our countryside so satisfying during the long weeks of winter.

All the same, evergreens do lose their foliage, but they shed leaves regularly and slowly at all times of the year, so we do not notice it.

You could make a collection of pressed leaves for your Collector Badge and include some of the brightest autumn colours.

**Geraldine Mellor**

# BROWNIES ROUND THE WORLD

### by Debbi Scholes

## Spain

In 1932, Spanish Boy Scout leaders were approached by groups of girls who wanted to join in with their activities. The leaders agreed to train the girls and in a short time Guide Companies were formed, followed by Brownie Packs and Ranger Units.

Brownies in Spain have different names depending on the area they live in. Catalonian Brownies are called Daina, while in the rest of Spain they are called Alita.

The Alita motto is 'Haremos lo megor' which means 'We shall do our best'. The motto of the Daina is 'Tant com puc' which means 'To do my best'.

Many people believe that it is hot and sunny all the time in Spain but, in fact, the climate changes in the different parts of Spain. However, when it is hot, the Spanish people spend their time differently from us in the UK. The midday meal for a typical family starts at about 2.00 pm and goes on until about 4.00 pm. Mealtimes are very important in many Continental countries, Spain included, as a time for chatting, and enjoying the food at a leisurely pace. As lunch finishes so late most families don't eat dinner until around 8.30 or 9.00 in the evening.

Spain's most famous dish is called paella. The basis of this is rice, coloured a pretty yellow with saffron, and mixed with a large variety of ingredients: chicken, ham, veal, tomato, peppers, green peas, and very often shell fish such as prawns and mussels.

One part of Spain, Andalusia, has a special soup called gazpacho which is so good that it is now eaten in all regions. To make gazpacho you will need:

¾ pt canned tomato juice
½ lb cucumber, peeled and grated
1 clove of garlic, skinned and chopped
2 tbsp olive oil
2 tbsp wine vinegar
sugar and salt to taste
chopped parsley

Mix all the ingredients together in a large bowl except the parsley. Chill in the refrigerator. Serve with the chopped parsley to garnish.

Vegetables have a short season in Spain. They are delicious while they last but the hot sun ripens them early in the year and they are soon shrivelled up. The climate in the south of Spain is very good for growing some of the fruits we find it difficult to grow in the UK such as oranges, lemons, peaches and grapes.

After lunch almost everyone has a siesta, a quiet time out of the sun in which to rest or sleep. All activities come to a halt for two or three hours and Spain comes to life again only around 6.00 in the evening. If you were to walk about during the siesta you might catch a glimpse of someone asleep under a tree, or in the shade of a balcony, any shelter they can find from the sun.

In the evening, when the air is cooler, many families stroll around the town or village, looking in the shops, which close during the siesta, greeting their friends, or sitting at tables outside cafés watching the world go by.

In many ways the Spanish people still lead an old-fashioned way of life. Much cooking is done on charcoal, even in houses which have electricity. In parts of the country, women still wash their clothes in the river, scrubbing them against large flat rocks to get them clean.

Most Spanish children are called after Saints and it is on the name day of their Saint that they receive presents and have parties, rather than on their birthday. Instead of hanging up a Christmas stocking on December 24th, Spanish children tie their shoes onto the balcony on January 6th, a day when traditionally the Three Kings visit all the houses and put gifts into the shoes.

# Greece

Brownies in Greece are called Poulis, which means birds, and their Promise Badge is a little gold bird. There have been Guides and Brownies in Greece for over 50 years. The Brownie Law in Greece is

*'A Brownie: obeys willingly:*
*Does not think only of herself:*
*Loves those around her'.*

Their motto is the same as ours, Lend a Hand. In Greek this is 'Dosse Kheri'.

The country of Greece is made up of the mainland and many islands scattered around; to be exact, 166 inhabited islands and 1,256 deserted ones.

In the summer the weather is very hot and sunny, so the people have a slightly different way of life from us. Greek children are normally in school by 8.00 am, coming home for lunch around 2.00 pm, and then resting in the afternoon. In many families the adults (and sometimes the children too) eat dinner at 10.00 pm and then perhaps go to a late night show at the open-air cinema.

In Greece children start school at the age of six. In some city schools classes are so large there are two sessions, with some children coming only in the morning and others just in the afternoon. In such cases, pupils may have extra homework to do when they are not at school.

As Greek families can spend much of their time out of doors in the sunshine, the houses need only be quite small. The living room is usually reserved for special occasions and guests. As the kitchens tend to be small too, people who live in the country often do their cooking outside, while in the towns Sunday lunch is sometimes prepared at home and then taken to be cooked in the large bread oven at the local baker's. It is not unusual to see someone walking up the road carrying a large baking tin full of moussaka or stuffed aubergines!

A simple and tasty dish to make which starts off many Greek meals is Tzatziki. To make it you will need:

½ pint of natural yoghurt
½ a cucumber, peeled and cut into small chunks
1 clove of garlic, peeled and finely sliced
a little fresh mint, chopped (dried will do)
½ tsp lemon juice
salt and black pepper

Mix all the ingredients together in a bowl, and serve it very cold as a dip for pieces of bread. If you can, try and use pitta bread — many supermarkets sell this.

A typical day's meals for a Greek family might be:
**Breakfast** A slice of bread, or a piece of plain cake and Greek coffee, which is strong, sweet and thick
**Mid-morning** Cheese pastries
**Lunch** A vegetable dish, or salad with bread
**Dinner** A fish or meat dish, with vegetables, salad and bread, followed by fresh fruit and/or pastries and cakes

A favourite pastime in Greece is dancing. Many restaurants and cafés (called tavernas) have live music played on an instrument called a bouzouki which looks rather like a mandolin. Many customers like to get up and dance the national dances which everyone learns as soon as they can walk. Sometimes the dancers and onlookers get so excited the plates are smashed in time to the music. The plates are usually specially reserved for this purpose, not ones taken from the tables!

# Italy

Italian Brownies are called Primulas or Cochinellas. The Primula is a pretty little flower, while the Cochinella is a ladybird. You can see this if you look at the Promise badges.

The motto of Italian Brownies is 'Fa meglio' which means 'Do better'.

Italy is very easy to find on the map, it looks just like a big boot about to kick a ball. The ball is the island of Sicily. Like the Spaniards and Greeks, the Italian people spend a lot of their time out of doors in the summer. Their restaurants and cafés are clubs for meeting people, as well as eating places, but mostly Italian families eat at home. Family life is very important to Italians, and they find most of their entertainment inside the home.

Wheat is an important crop in Italy, to provide the pasta which is the main food item. Pasta is made in a wide variety of shapes and sizes. The three best known to us are macaroni, spaghetti and vermicelli. The last means 'little worms' and describes its shape very well. Anyone not used to eating pasta would probably cut up these three pastas to eat them, but the Italians twist the strands round and round a fork, right up to the handle, then eat the huge forkful at once! These types of pasta are served with sauces and Parmesan cheese. Other forms of pasta have fillings of meat or vegetables, for example ravioli and cannelloni.

Pizza is another very popular dish in Italy. Here is a way to make a cheat's pizza. You will need:

1 small size French loaf, about 12" long
4 oz grated cheese
1 small tin of tomatoes
2 tsps tomato purée
8 slices of salami or ham
oil, salt and pepper

Cut the loaf in half longways, then cut each half in half again, to make four bases. Brush each piece of bread with a little oil. Drain the tomatoes then put them in a bowl and mash them up. Add the tomato purée and salt and pepper and mix well. Spread a thin layer of this onto each piece of bread, put the slices of ham or salami on top and the grated cheese onto this. Put the 'pizzas' onto a baking tray and place in the oven at gas mark 4/190°C/375°F. Bake them for about 10 minutes until the cheese has melted and the bread is crispy. Serve with a green salad. You can vary pizza by adding any of the following: black or green olives, anchovies, sliced green pepper, onions or mushrooms.

Italian meals may start off with all sorts of small dishes, such as olives, tuna fish, prawns, parma ham, and melon. Fish is plentiful, coming from both the sea and lakes. Italian cheeses are excellent, with many different flavours, from the creamy Bel Paese to the very hard Parmesan. Many are made from the milk of sheep or goats, giving them a very distinctive taste. Mozzarella, which is usually used on pizzas, is traditionally made from buffalo milk!

Because of the heat in the summer, Italians have a siesta in the afternoon, until it is cool enough to go out on the street or back to work. In a large city like Rome, the streets become very dusty during the summer months, so water-spraying trucks go around wetting the dust, to prevent it blowing about when the wind springs up at dusk.

There are many festivals associated with religion in Italy. Processions and festivals are held to mark many of the Saints' days. Sometimes the festivals celebrate the changing seasons of the year, such as seed-time and harvest, which are so important to people who work on the land.

Many Italian festivals are held to recall the atmosphere of olden days. In Florence each year, a game of football takes place in which all the players wear the costume of the sixteenth century.

# PUZZLE PAGE

**devised by Brenda Apsley**

## Brownie Badge Puzzle

Here's a crossword with a difference. Identify each of the Interest Badge symbols, and fit the names into the Brownie Badge grid. Your *Brownie Guide Handbook* will help you!

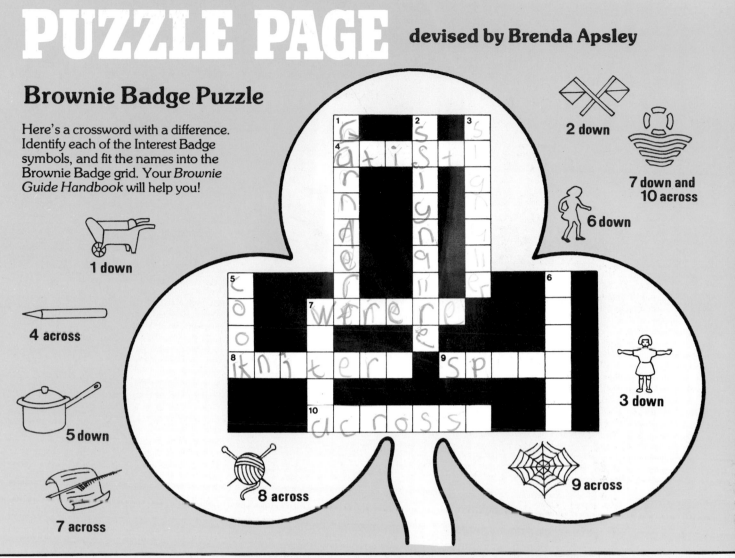

**1 down**

**4 across**

**5 down**

**7 across**

**8 across**

**2 down**

**7 down and 10 across**

**6 down**

**3 down**

**9 across**

## A Pie Puzzle

Ann has baked an apple pie in the shape of a triangle. How must she cut it so that she, and her friends Barbara and Carol, get equal-sized pieces and there's none left over? Try different cuts on a piece of scrap paper.

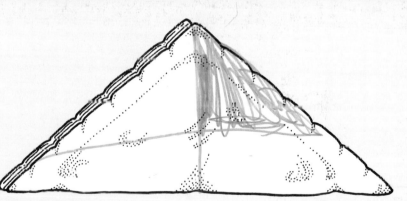

## A Pair Puzzle

Alison the Brownie was on Pack Holiday. She had white socks and fawn socks in her suitcase, and had to find a matching pair, but it was still dark, and she couldn't see what colour the socks were! How many socks did she take out to be sure of a matching pair?

Solutions on page 61.

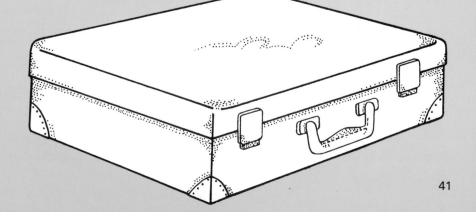

# THE ADVENT WREATH

## by Natalie Webber

By the end of the Brownie meeting on Saturday morning it was snowing hard. Kirsten looked out of the Meeting Hall windows at the huge flakes floating past and her heart sank. She knew she wouldn't be allowed to go skiing with the boys that afternoon. If the snow went on her mother would say it was too dangerous. And there would be no point in arguing.

"When you can ski as well as your brothers . . ."

They'd had the argument so many times she knew it by heart. New snow was treacherous unless you were a good skier and Kirsten was only a reasonable skier. So, no skiing on fresh snow. What a waste of a Saturday!

Kirsten glared at nothing in particular, but was suddenly woken from her thoughts by the Leader, calling out their Brownie motto, as she did at the end of every meeting: "Freudig Helfen!" — "Help Joyfully!"

And they all called back, as they did every week, "Freudig Helfen!"

But Kirsten didn't feel very joyful, and she pulled on her boots and anorak and trudged through the village without waiting for her friends. The mountains were hidden by the falling snow and all the shops were lit as though it was night-time. Her moon boots made a dull thud on the pavement with each step, and the snow kept piling up on her nose and having to be wiped off.

illustrated by Hilary Mullock

She pushed open the chalet door and took off her boots and wet clothes in the drying room under the house. Then she thumped up the stairs to the living room and bumped into her mother.

"Goodness, what a cross face!" said her mother.

"Well, it's snowing." Kirsten knew her mother hated whining and waited to be ticked off.

But her mother smiled. "Better things to do than skiing this afternoon. Have you forgotten what tomorrow is?"

Kirsten thought. Four weeks to Christmas, Sunday tomorrow. Light suddenly dawned and the whole day cheered up in a flash.

"It's Advent tomorrow," she shouted. "The first Sunday in Advent! There's the wreath to make and the candle to get out and — can we start *now*?"

Her mother grinned at her. "Be a bit patient. Your father is out getting the evergreen for you, because the weather is so bad. Come and have your omelette and by the time you've finished he'll be back."

True enough, at the end of lunch her father staggered into the kitchen, nearly buried under an armful of evergreen from the garden. He dumped it on the table and looked at Kirsten. "Over to you," he said, and disappeared again.

Kirsten and her mother set to work. While Kirsten snipped small pieces of evergreen from the bigger branches, her mother made a circle of crumpled

42

chicken wire, about fifty centimetres across.

"Isn't it nice to think," said Kirsten, "that all over Austria families are making wreaths for Advent, just like us."

"Not every family does it any more," her mother replied. "When I was small, everyone made them and some of them were huge, as big as cart wheels."

When the ring was ready, Kirsten found the bag of moss her father had brought in, and pushed it into the holes in the wire, until there was moss all round the circle.

"Now the candles!" she shouted, and four red candles were pushed into the wire, and then four lengths of red ribbon tied on, to hang the wreath from the ceiling.

Together they did the most difficult part. The twigs of ivy and evergreens had to be pushed into the moss, until the whole wreath was covered.

"And tomorrow," Kirsten said happily, "we'll light one candle, and read the gospel for the first Sunday in Advent, and next Sunday we'll light *two* candles, and read the gospel for the second . . ."

"But *now* it's getting dark," her mother interrupted. "Aren't you going to get the big candle out?"

The best bit of all! Kirsten leapt up and hauled the kitchen bench over to the tall cupboard, to get to the shelf where the huge Advent candle was kept. She stood it in its holder and then carried it very carefully up to the landing.

"*Why* do we light the big candle for Advent?" she asked, as she did every year, just to hear her mother tell the story again.

"Well, the legend says that the candle in the window will guide the Christchild to the house in time for Christmas. So we light it every evening as it

gets dark, so that He can find the way when He comes."

"He's going to *need* a candle if this snow goes on," said Kirsten fervently.

"It's only a story." Her mother smiled at her.

Kirsten looked out at the darkness and the snow falling and falling like a great net curtain. Even if it *is* only a story, she thought, I'm *glad* we lit a candle for Him!

If you make a wreath like Kirsten's, it is safer to stand it on a tin tray than to try to hang it up. And be *very* careful to keep the greenery much lower than the tops of the candles.

# MAKING FACES!

GIRL GUIDES

**by Debbi Scholes**

## You will need:

A balloon (or two in case one pops)
Vaseline or petroleum jelly
About 8 tbsp flour
water
tissue paper torn into strips
newspapers
plain paper
glue, string, sticky tape
paint
an overall or apron
paper-clip

First blow up the balloon until it is a little larger than your head and tie a knot in the end. Ask for help with this if you can't manage it. Then secure the tied end to a plate with a strip of sticky tape. Cover the balloon with a very thin layer of the Vaseline or petroleum jelly to protect it while you work.

To make the flour paste, mix 8 tablespoonsful of flour with just under a half pint of water and stir until you have a fairly runny paste.

Dip small strips of tissue into the paste (do not make it too wet) and cover the balloon. This will give you a good surface to work on. Tear your newspapers into pieces about 2 inches square very roughly (making sure they aren't today's papers), dip them into the paste one by one and lay on the balloon. Continue doing this until you have covered the tissue, then begin another layer. When you have finished a couple of layers it is a good idea to paint quickly over the paper so you can see that you are covering the balloon evenly.

After about 15 layers, the papier mâché should be thick enough, so you must leave your balloon to dry very thoroughly. When dry it should feel hard if you rap it with your knuckles.

Now, for the next step, make sure that your Mum and, particularly, any pets are out of the room, because you must pop the balloon by cutting off the knot at the bottom.

Then, with a pair of scissors, cut the balloon in half, starting at the open end where the knot was. Now you have two masks to decorate as you wish.

Perhaps one could be made into a witch's mask, in which case you will need to make a hooked nose, an evil toothless grin and hooded

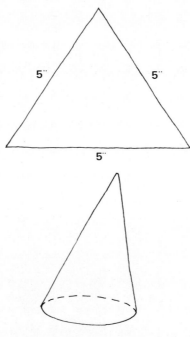

eyes. Start with the nose. Cut out a triangle of stiffish paper, 5" by 5" by 5". Roll two sides together to make a cone shape and glue the edges down.

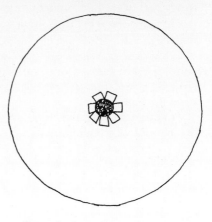

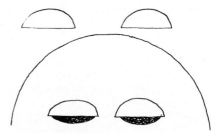

Cut a hole in the centre of your mask, just big enough to stick the larger end of the cone through, snip around the edge of the paper cone, bend the snipped edges back and glue the mask. The eyes can be two slits cut into the mask, but first rest the mask against your face and lightly touch the places where you think they should be

with a pen. Then to give her a wicked, hooded look, cut out two pieces of paper like half closed eyelids and stick across the top of the eye holes.

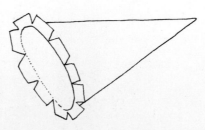

Witches are usually pictured as having only half their teeth, so you could cut out an uneven set of teeth in a huge evil mouth.

At this stage you can paint your mask any weird colours that you may think would suit a witch, perhaps green!

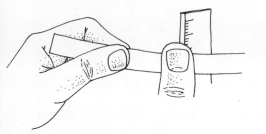

To make hair for the witch you need 8 strips of paper, painted black, measuring ½" x 10". Very carefully hold the end of a strip of paper between the thumb and finger of one hand and run the strip in between your thumb and the edge of a ruler or pencil a few times, until the paper begins to curl. Don't tug too hard on the paper or it will tear. Stick one end of these strands of hair to the witch's head, letting it fall like hair.

Punch two holes, one each side of your mask, just above your ears. Cut two pieces of string, each long enough to go half-way around your head, tie a knot in one end of each piece and thread the strings through the holes. These should tie at the back of your head.

Lastly, your witch needs a hat. Cut out a circle of stiff black paper, 12" in diameter, cut out one quarter of the circle and pull the two cut edges together to make another cone. When it is pointed enough for a witch's hat, glue the two edges together using a paper clip to hold them firm while the glue is drying.

To make the brim, cut out a circle of the same paper 1½" wider than the bottom of the cone. Inside this circle, draw another one, 2" smaller, and cut it out. Push the cone through this circle, snip the edges as you did on the nose and

bend back onto the brim and glue. Now you have your witch's hat, ready to go onto your head when you are wearing the mask.

The other mask is up to you, use your imagination, and have fun!

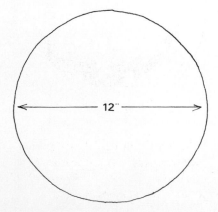

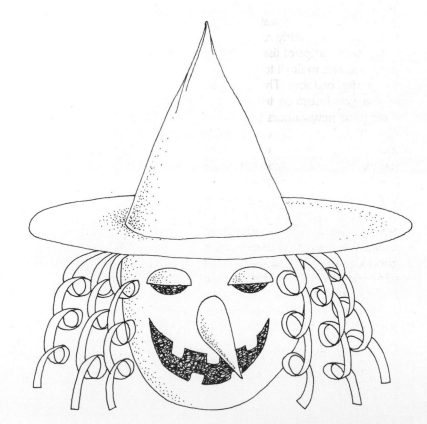

drawn by Chris Sheridan

# CONSERVATION BADGE

Conservation is all about looking after things, about protecting wild life and the countryside and taking care not to waste the earth's resources.

Because of the wasteful way we live we are thoughtlessly polluting rivers and oceans and pumping smoke and chemicals into the air. In some places the land is already so polluted that it will not allow any plants to grow. Elsewhere, so much rubbish has been put into the rivers that all the fish have died.

The planet earth is like a giant spaceship travelling through space. Everything that we need to live must be carried on board. Our supplies are limited and once we run out of anything, we will never be able to replace it.

Everything in nature is in balance. Plants use the sun to make food; animals like rabbits eat the plants; other animals like foxes eat the animals which eat the plants. This is called a food chain. If any part of it is changed, other plants and animals will be affected. When we disturb the balance of nature we harm ourselves because we are part of nature.

The pollution of the countryside first started with the Industrial Revolution in the early 1700s. The burning coal produced thick black smoke which began to kill plants and animals in the countryside and damage people's health in the cities. Since then over 200 different kinds of plants and animals have died out. Once we lose a certain type of animal, it is gone for ever.

Our towns and cities spread over more and more of the countryside leaving less space for wild animals and plants. Farmers make bigger fields in an attempt to grow food more economically, but in so doing they pull up and destroy hedges and banks which are the habitat of many birds and beasts.

We can help to stop this process by creating small areas where our native wildlife will thrive. If you have a garden, leave a small patch of weeds or nettles, as butterflies and other insects lay their eggs on these. You can help birds through the winter by regularly putting out food for them. A good mixture of different foods will bring a variety of birds; sunflower and other seeds, bacon rind and peanuts are all good. When deciding on a feeding place, choose one that is safe from cats.

Many harmless plants are killed by weed killers, which contain chemicals that spread over the ground. Some people will spray hedges and banks with weed killer because they are too lazy to cut the plants back. Other chemicals are used to kill insects that live in the garden and on crops. These insecticides are often harmful not only to the insects but also to the birds and animals that feed on the insects.

It is not only wildlife that needs looking after. We use and throw away tons of natural resources each year. There is only a limited supply of metal, wood, and stone in the world, and if we use it only

**by Sally J. Hyman**

# SPACESHIP "EARTH"

once and then throw it away we will soon run out. Every household in Britain throws away one tonne of rubbish each year, which comes to 16 million tonnes of rubbish overall. This is extremely wasteful, as much of this rubbish could be used again. Many things like tin cans and glass bottles can be melted down and used to make new cans and bottles.

Using things again in this way is called recycling. Cloth, paper and even oil can be recycled. Have you seen the recycling symbol on anything?

Sometimes Guides and Rangers collect newspapers or cloth and sell them to recycling firms. This not only helps with conservation but also makes money for Guide funds. In some towns bottle banks and places to take old tins are being started. You take your empty bottles, jars and cans there and they are melted down to make new ones.

You can recycle things yourself, by making further use of them. Old coffee jars make good storage jars, and pots with air tight lids can be used for storage or as plant pots. Pieces of material can be used in patchwork and many useful and pretty things can be made from scraps and oddments. Even waste vegetables can be recycled if you have a garden. If you compost them, in a few months you will have a thick brown compost which will fertilize the garden soil.

We need energy to heat and light our homes, for cooking, to make our cars and lorries go, and for factories. We get most of our energy from burning oil, petrol, gas and coal, which are called fossil fuels. The trouble is that we have already used up a good deal of these fossil fuels and eventually we will not have any left. We can get energy from wind power, from wave power, from the sun and from nuclear power stations, but scientists and engineers need time to find the best ways of getting energy from these recently discovered sources, so we must make the best use of our fossil fuels and make sure they last long enough.

When we are cooking we should try not to waste energy by only putting one thing in the oven at a time. We should cover saucepans with lids and put different vegetables in the same pan to cook. Even things like keeping doors closed or drawing the curtains as soon as it gets dark in the winter will save a little heat energy, and we should always make sure that we turn lights off when we have finished using them.

It is everybody's responsibility to look after the earth, its plants and its creatures, and to make it a better place to live in. Why don't you find out what you can do in your area, and work towards the Conservation Badge?

**Illustrated by Sheila Edwards** 47

This photo shows Brian talking to Marie watched by Penny and Lucy, with Natalie and the editor in the background.

# IT'S A WINNER!

Did you enter the competition in the 1982 Brownie Annual? We asked you to send in a painting or drawing of your Brownie Pack and received hundreds of marvellous pictures. After the closing date of the competition we carefully sorted out the best fifty, and then invited Brian Sanders to come and judge them.

Brian is the artist who painted the pictures of Guides, Brownies, Scouts, Cubs, the Boys' Brigade and the Girls' Brigade which were used on the special commemorative stamps issued in 1982. He was very impressed by the high standard of all the entries and found it most difficult to choose the winners but, in the end, the first prize went to Penny Davies of 11th Ipswich Brownie Pack for her lively drawing of a Pack meeting.

The runners-up were Marie Peppercorn of 7th Oldham Brownie Pack, and Lucy Woollatt of 1st Grimston Brownie Pack.

These three Brownies, along with their Mums and Dads, were invited to come to Guide Headquarters to be presented with their prizes. So one day during the school holidays Penny, Marie and Lucy, their Mums, Dads, brothers and sisters, even grannies and aunties, all came up to London and found their way to Buckingham Palace Road.

First we took them on a guided tour of headquarters, finishing up in the Council Chamber where a display of the best pictures had been arranged. We then held a short ceremony to present the prizes, which were donated by Reeves Paints. Brian congratulated the Brownies and, as an extra prize, gave them each a first day cover of the special stamps. Then Natalie Webber, the Brownie consultant to the Programme Adviser, who was representing Lady Baden-Powell, presented the Brownies with certificates and added her congratulations. Then we all had tea!

This drawing was by Penny Davies
of 11th Ipswich Brownie Pack

We had so many entries it was very
difficult to choose the best.
All the pictures that didn't win
were passed to the editor of the
Brownie Magazine, so perhaps you
will see your drawing on the
'All my own' page one day.

Are you going to enter this year's
competition?
See page 61 for details.

Runner-up
Marie Peppercorn painted this picture

Runner-up
This picture was drawn by Lucy Woollatt

# Frogs and Toads

## written and illustrated by John Norris Wood

There are only three species of frogs and toads which are native to Britain: the Common Frog, the Common Toad, and the much rarer Natterjack Toad. Some other species, such as the Marsh Frog and the Edible Frog, have been introduced from Europe, and have formed colonies in a few suitable areas.

Many people have difficulty in telling a frog from a toad, but with our British ones the differences are quite clear. The frog has a smooth, moist skin which gives it a shiny appearance, while the toad's skin is drier and rougher looking, covered with lots of small bumps. The more streamlined frog has longer back legs in proportion to its body than the more heavily built and squat toad. Frogs leap and move faster altogether, while the Common Toad moves mainly by walking, only hopping when startled.

The colours of frogs and toads will not help you much to tell one from the other as they vary greatly, but Common Frogs have a dark patch on either side of their heads, which you can see in the photograph.

Frogs and toads are very dependant on water. They don't drink through their mouths but by absorbing water through their skins.

Both frogs, and especially toads, can defend themselves by releasing irritating secretions from glands in their skins, which taste very nasty to any animal that picks them up in its mouth. These secretions can sting if you get them in a cut or into your eyes. Frogs and toads dislike being handled, so if you *have* to pick one up be very gentle indeed.

**Common Frog**

**Common Toad**

**Natterjack Toad**

**Hands of male frog and toad in Spring showing rough pads**

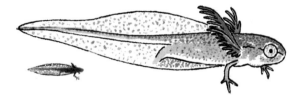

1. Spawn 2. About three weeks later, a few days later, a few days after hatching, anchored to the jelly, feeding on the yolk 3. Mouth appears a few days later, it breathes through gills like a fish and feeds on algae 4. Gills absorbed back into body and become lungs, so tadpole now breathes air from the surface 5. Hind limbs appear, tadpole now eats animal food, eg dead fish 6. front limbs developing 7. About twelve weeks after hatching the tadpole has all its legs 8. It absorbs its tail back into its body as

food and must now eat large numbers of tiny insects. After about three years it will be fully adult and able to breed.

**Marsh Frog**

This is a newt tadpole. The front feet develop first at a very early stage. The small drawing shows the actual size six weeks after hatching.

In the early Spring our amphibians seek out suitable ponds to breed in. At this time of year you can tell which are the male frogs and toads as they develop special rough pads on their hands which help them to clasp the females during breeding. They become very noisy at this time, the Common Frogs make a soft purring kind of croak, while the toads have a high trilling call. The frogs pair up and produce a clump of spawn containing thousands of eggs. The toads produce long strings of spawn which are woven in and out of the water weeds.

The time the eggs take to hatch depends on the temperature of the water; cold weather slows things down. The pictures explain the stages the tadpoles go through. If you rear tadpoles the main points to remember are to use pond water, never to overcrowd — have only a few, say twelve in a goldfish bowl. Feed them sparingly with a good standard make of *tropical* fish food, and don't forget to provide a piece of cork bark for the froglets to climb on to. Finally, always let them go in the undergrowth near an unpolluted pond immediately they reach the stage (number 8) in the pictures. It isn't possible for you to provide the masses of minute, different insects that are essential for their welfare. Once their front legs appear the tank or bowl should be covered with a ventilated top so they can't escape. If they get out into a room they will dry up and die in a very short time.

**Edible Frog**

**Edible Frog**

Frogs and toads are cold blooded animals, which means they are the same temperature as their surroundings. They are most active in the warmer weather when their insect food is plentiful. In the winter they hibernate away from frost, frogs usually at the bottom of ponds, and toads in sheltered places on the ground.

Frogs and toads feed only on living prey, eating a great number of beetles, caterpillars, grubs, ants, slugs and small snails, in fact almost anything they can cram into their large mouths. They are rightly called the gardener's friends.

The best way to help our amphibians is to provide them with a special pond in an undisturbed place, where it will receive some sunlight and is not directly under trees. Do not include fish as they will eat tadpoles. You will need help from an adult with the digging, as part of the pond must be at least two feet deep and it must have a shelf or shallow part about five inches deep. Make it as large as you can.

A few clay soils hold water naturally, but you will probably need to line your pool with a thick gauge piece of plastic, or better still, butyl, from a garden centre or aquarist's shop. A lined or concrete pool will need a drain.

You will need several special plastic baskets for the submerged waterweeds. Fill them with ordinary soil, and don't forget to plant reeds, rushes and marginal plants around the edge to provide plenty of cover. Put lots of stones in the shallow water so it is not too slippery for creatures to climb in and out. Last, but not least, ask an adult to help you put a secure fence around the pond so that small children cannot fall in.

There are about three thousand different kinds of frogs and toads and they are found all over the world except in the driest and coldest regions. In order to survive they have developed amazing shapes, colours and patterns, and evolved many fascinating ways of living.

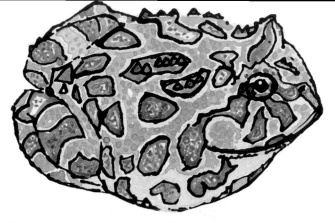

The Argentine Horned Frog is a large and powerful amphibian with very sharp teeth. It will not hesitate to drive off animals much larger than itself. This drawing is of a young frog.

There are frogs which are perfectly adapted to life in the trees, with heavily webbed, parachute-like hands and feet to help them glide through the air. Some kinds have specially formed feet to burrow into the ground, while others spend their whole life in water and have huge hind flippers, like frogmen! Some species are very poisonous and have brilliantly coloured skin to warn off predators. Many frogs have camouflaged skin perfectly matching their surroundings, and are able to change their colour to some extent.

Most frogs and toads are quite timid, but a few, such as the African Bullfrog, are quite fierce and can draw blood with their sharp teeth. Another called the Dagger Frog can inflict wounds with a sharp bone in its thumbs.

But perhaps the frog's strangest behaviour is shown while protecting its young. The male Poison Arrow Frog becomes a walking nursery, carrying the tadpoles on his back. The tiny Darwin's Frog swallows the eggs, which develop inside his vocal sacs, finally hopping out of his mouth as complete froglets! Some frogs build special little nursery pools for their tadpoles; others make foamy nests in trees overhanging water. The male Midwife Toad winds the strings of eggs around his back legs and takes them to hatch in the water. Some species have special pits or pouches on their backs where the eggs can develop safe from enemies until they wriggle out as tiny frogs.

This Green Tree Frog comes from coastal rainforests in Australia. When it closes its brilliant eyes it seems almost to disappear among the leaves.

It is not difficult to see why the Tomato Frog got its popular name! It is a rarely seen species from Madagascar.

Probably the first loud voice heard on earth many millions of years ago belonged to a frog-like creature. Many frogs and toads are good singers, often forming great choruses during the breeding season, which can be quite deafening, and heard from far away. Usually the males make these sounds with their mouths closed. They pump air back and forth over various balloon-like vocal sacs, which act rather like bagpipes! Different species often have distinct calls, some sounding like dogs barking, or rattles, burps, screams, snorts, grunts, moans, cows mooing, birds singing, bells, hammers and even machinery. Some frogs are an extraordinary sight when calling as they have vocal sacs which when inflated are almost as big as themselves. There are records available of frogs calling; see if you can listen to one.

The very strange shape and camouflage of the Asian Leaf Frog blends perfectly with the fallen leaves of the jungle.

This drawing of Darwin's Frog is like an X-ray showing a few of the tadpoles inside the male's vocal sac, almost ready to hop out. This tiny frog comes from Chile and Argentina.

The elegant Hoses Frog from the East Indies is beautifully marked to blend in with its surroundings.

The brilliant colours of the South American Poison Arrow Frog show that it has deadly poisons in its skin. Some Indians put this poison on their arrow tips. The African Clawed Frog is perfectly adapted to spending its whole life in water. It has funny little lidless eyes, huge flippers and a *very* slippery skin. It makes a noise like a sewing machine!

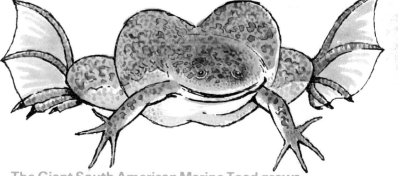

The Giant South American Marine Toad grows up to nine inches. It eats an enormous quantity of insects and has been imported into many tropical countries to protect sugar cane crops from pests! If alarmed it puffs itself up, as in the picture.

One sunny September morning the Brownies of 2nd Bushey Grove and 13th Bushey Packs set off for Beechwood, the South West Hertfordshire camp site, to be Pirates for the day. They wore moustaches, eye patches, stripey jerseys and boots, and were armed to the teeth with swords, daggers and cutlasses!

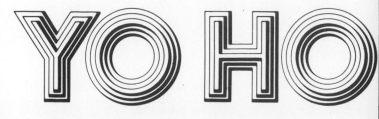

## Pack Holiday Pirates

First job on arrival was to make the boats for the Pirates to sail.

Next the Pirates made skull-and-crossbones flags to fly from the masts.

The field began to look more like an ocean as the sails of the Pirate fleet fluttered in the breeze. Each ship had an impressive figurehead.

Each Pirate brought along a parrot made at an earlier Pack Meeting. This one preferred to perch on a tree stump!

# HO!

## by Frank and Joan Randall

The Jolly Rogers looked rather fearsome as they took shape.

A couple of fierce Pirates stopped work for a chat.

The Pirates queued up to receive their rations.

When the weather grew stormy the Pirates hurried into harbour (the wet weather hut), where they sang sea shanties, including *My ship sailed from China*.

The sun came out again and it was time to walk the plank. Luckily no one fell into the shark-infested sea!

By the end of the day most of the Pirates had grown beards! Here they are gathered together to sing *Fifteen men on a deadman's chest, Yo ho ho and a bottle of rum!*

A few Pirates took to fighting.

# PUZZLE PAGE

devised by Lesley Scott

## What a Muddle!

Katie has packed her suitcase all
ready to go on Pack Holiday with
her Brownie Pack, but everything
has been muddled up inside!
Can you help Katie sort her things
out?

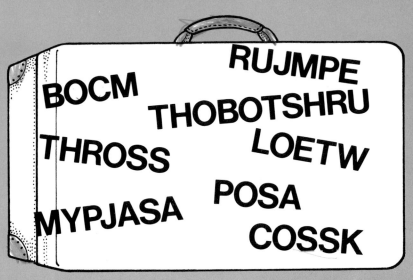

BOCM
RUJMPE
THOBOTSHRU
THROSS
LOETW
MYPJASA
POSA
COSSK

## Famous Books

How much do you know about books — and the
people who wrote them? Here are some very
famous books you will know straight away.
But do you know who wrote them?

LITTLE WOMEN

The Wind in the Willows

ROBINSON CRUSOE 3.

Alice in Wonderland 4.

THE TALE OF PETER RABBIT 5.

## Collective Nouns

Collective nouns are the words that describe a group
of things, for example, a *flock* of sheep. Get the
picture? Right! Now, here's the puzzle! Do you know
the collective nouns for these groups of things?

1 A _ _ _ _ of elephants

2 A _ _ _ _ _ of fish

3 A _ _ _ _ _ _ _ of kittens

4 A _ _ _ _ _ _ of geese

5 A _ _ _ _ _ of lions

6 A _ _ _ _ _ of foxes

7 A _ _ _ _ of wolves

8 A _ _ _ _ _ of bees

Solutions on page 61.

# The White Elephant Stall

We must have the biggest Brownie hut in the world. Well, it's not a hut really, it's an old school. You know, one of those that was built years and years ago. Mind you, it's not been used as a school for ages. We like it because it's got great high ceilings and lots of odd little corners. If you go into one of these new schools you can nearly touch the ceiling if you stand on a chair, and the rooms are all the same.

In our Brownie hut there are so many rooms and storage cupboards that some of them have not been opened up for years. Janice Hudson said that it would be a fantastic place to play hide and seek because no one would ever find you. I don't think that's true, but Mrs Colvin, our Brown Owl, says that the younger members of the Pack are not allowed on the top floor because it would take all night to get them back together again!

Mrs Colvin's great. She has introduced us to all sorts of new activities. My favourite was the week we went on Pack Holiday in Yorkshire. Talk about being different from Clayton! I couldn't get over how green everything was. Clayton's nice but it's in the middle of a big city and it certainly isn't very green. When we got back Brown Owl made Janice and Adele tell the whole Pack about the holiday. Janice made everyone laugh when she described how Barbara Toland's camp bed collapsed, and then Barbara made everyone laugh even more when she told us how Janice came rushing in saying she'd been chased by a bull! It was really one of Mr Rawson's cows!

It was because we enjoyed the holiday so much that Brown Owl suggested we should hold an Autumn Fair and Jumble Sale. We wanted to raise enough money to go away again next year so some of those who missed out this year could go too. Janice, Adele and I volunteered to run the white elephant stall. I said there wasn't really much call for white elephants in Clayton and Mrs Colvin laughed, and explained that a white elephant stall sells things like ornaments and fancy goods. We had three weeks to collect lots of items before the Fair.

The following week on our way to Brownies we met Mrs Colvin. She asked us how the collecting was going.

"Not so good, Miss," Janice answered.

"You can say that again," I added. "Who'd believe that after a whole week we've only got nine things?"

"That's not too bad," Mrs Colvin said encouragingly.

"Three chipped flying ducks, two bells without clappers, two glass clowns, one ash tray, and a metal thing that we don't even know what it is, from Janice's grandad," I said.

By the next week we had added two matching white china dogs, another ash try, and Janice's grandad had donated another metal thing that matched the first. We still didn't know what they were. It looked as though our stall was going to be a real disaster. As we approached the Brownie hut with our disheartening news Adele suddenly grabbed hold of Janice and me. "Look, I know where we can get lots of items for our stall!" she said.

Janice and I jumped up and down with excitement. "Where? Where?"

"Well you know Wayne Denny and those lads that collect bottles?"

"Yes," we replied.

"Well, I know where they get them from. They dig

58

**by Howard Tennant**

drawn by Chris Sheridan

them up," said Adele.

Behind our Brownie hut there's an old railway embankment that used to take the goods train to the head of the old Clayton coalmine. It hadn't been used for years, not since the pit closed. When the embankment was built back in the old days, the builders must have used all sorts of rubbish to build it up. A couple of years ago someone found a very old bottle there, and within a few days the embankment looked like Grandad's allotment on a sunny Sunday. There were people digging everywhere.

At first quite a few bottles were found and you could sell them for about a pound each. They were green and had a glass marble in the neck instead of a bottle top. But the supply soon ran out and most of the bottles were chipped or broken anyway. You could still find one or two bottles but you had to dig for ages, and besides, the police had put up a notice saying the embankment was dangerous. Some boys still went digging on the far side where you couldn't be seen from the road, but most people stayed away.

"You're not suggesting we go and dig for bottles, are you?" I asked Adele.

"Can you think of anything else?" Adele replied. "If we dig for long enough we'll find plenty of bottles for our stall."

We thought about it, as we desperately wanted to get some more things for our stall, but in the end I said: "Look, we're doing this for Brownies, aren't we? It would be stupid to go and dig when we know it's dangerous and we're not supposed to go there. Brown Owl would be really disappointed in us."

Janice and Adele nodded in agreement and we trudged into the Brownie meeting feeling fed up.

"Come on you three," said Brown Owl. "We've got plenty to do tonight. You can start by bringing down some tables from room 13 on the top floor. Here's the key. Don't be long and call out if you need any help."

We climbed the stairs, all three of us with our eyes on the floor as we thought about the few items for our stall.

Janice unlocked the door and flicked the light switch, but nothing happened.

"Oh, come on," I said. "There's enough light from the corridor. We can manage."

I felt my way into the dark room and my fingers touched what felt like a table top.

"Come and give a hand," I called, "there's a table." And I gave a strong pull.

I nearly jumped out of my skin when, instead of the table moving, there was the sound of glass rattling and clinking.

"What on earth was that?" asked Janice, still standing by the door. "Hey," she said, "this is the wrong room. It's 12, not 13. Come on out."

But by now my eyes were accustomed to the murky gloom and I could see that what I had thought was a table was an old wooden chest. I lifted up the lid and there inside were dozens and dozens of old ttles!

Brown Owl reckoned that the bottles were nearly as old as the school, and after checking with the owners of the hut that it was OK, we were allowed to sell them on our stall.

We made more money than any other stall, so next year we're going on Pack Holiday again, all of us. I can't wait for the summer to come. I wonder if the fields will be as green as I remember them?

# Oh! Christmas Tree

illustrations by Chris Sheridan

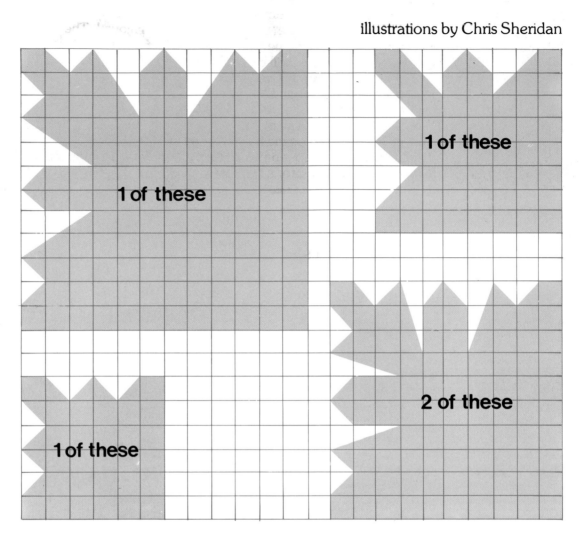

1 of these

1 of these

2 of these

1 of these

Make this pretty little tree using white, green or silver paper.

First place your fancy paper under this page and prick the pattern through, unless you want a larger tree, in which case you will have to transfer the pattern to larger graph paper. Don't forget you need 2 layers of the second largest size.

Now draw the patterns by joining the pin pricks.

Cut out each shape as a full square, then fold it in half diagonally so you can trim the edges of two sides at a time.

Now crease each shape along the other diagonal; fold it twice more to make creases joining the other four points.

Turn each shape over and fold it 4 times to make creases along lines joining the inward points.

To assemble, make a small hole in the centre of each layer, and thread them largest first smallest last, onto a slim drinking straw or a stick.

Stand the straw in a cotton reel, covered to lool like a tub, space the layers and arrange them decoratively. Make a star for the top.

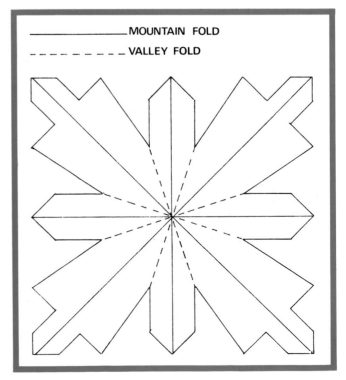

——————— MOUNTAIN FOLD
- - - - - - - VALLEY FOLD

# COMPETITION

Brownies — can you write a poem or story? We would like you to send us something you have written by yourself. It could be a poem, or a story, or a report of a Brownie event you particularly enjoyed. The prizes for the best entries include pens, personal writing paper and a children's encyclopaedia, and winning entries will be published in *The Brownie Annual*.

Send your entry to: The Editor, *The Brownie Annual*, 17-19 Buckingham Palace Road, London SW1W OPT.

Don't forget to write your name, address, age and Brownie Pack on your entry, and also tell me the three items you like best in this Annual. This is very important as it helps me to make the next Annual even better!

The closing date for entries is March 31st 1984. The winners will be notified by post and the Editor's decision is final.

# ANSWERS

**Puzzle Page** (page 16)

### CROSSWORD

**Across:** 1. Pow wow 6. Hoe 7. Cook 8. Elves 10. Sew 12. Lend 14. Serve 15. Tool 16. Gardener

**Down:** 1. Packs 2. Woodwork 3. Wool 4. Shoe 5. Web 9. Venture 11. Bulbs 12. Let 13. Do 14. Sing

### WORD PUZZLE 1

1. Highway 2. Six 3. (across) Arrow 3. (down) Ark 4. Thinking 5. Imps 6. Revels 7. Craft 8. Road 9. Sprites 10. Irish 11. Trails.

### WORD PUZZLE 2

1. Ingredients 2. Gnomes 3. Toadstool 4. Compass 5. Patrol 6. Foot 7. Collectors 8. (across) Cyclist 8. (down) Cup 9. SOS 10. Help 11. Twist

### Nature Quiz (page 17)

| | |
|---|---|
| 1 A Bumble Bee | 9 True |
| 2 A Mussel shell | 10 The Common Oak |
| 3 An Adder | 11 2,000 |
| 4 True | 12 The Blue Whale |
| 5 The Lombardy Poplar | 13 True |
| 6 African | 14 8 |
| 7 69 | 15 False |
| 8 Syria | |

### WORDSQUARE (page 31)

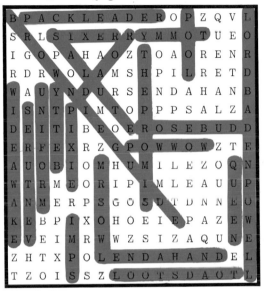

### A Page of Puzzles (page 41)

### BROWNIE BADGE PUZZLE

Down: 1 Gardener; 2 Signaller; 3 Athlete; 5 Cook; 6 Skater; 7 Water.

Across: 4 Artist; 7 Writer; 8 Knitter; 9 Craft; 10 Rescuer

### A PIE PUZZLE

To cut the pie into three equal pieces Ann must make cuts like this:

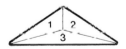

### A PAIR PUZZLE

Alison must take out three socks.

### A Page of Puzzles (page 57)

### WHAT A MUDDLE!

Torch; Boots; Socks; Shorts; Soap; Toothbrush; Jumper; Comb; Pyjamas; Towel.

### COLLECTIVE NOUNS

1 Herd; 2 Shoal; 3 Kindle; 4 Gaggle; 5 Pride; 6 Skulk; 7 Pack; 8 Swarm

### FAMOUS BOOKS

1. Louisa M Alcott; 2. Kenneth Grahame; 3. Daniel Defoe; 4. Lewis Carroll; 5. Beatrix Potter.

# BROWNIE GAME
**devised by Ann Martin**

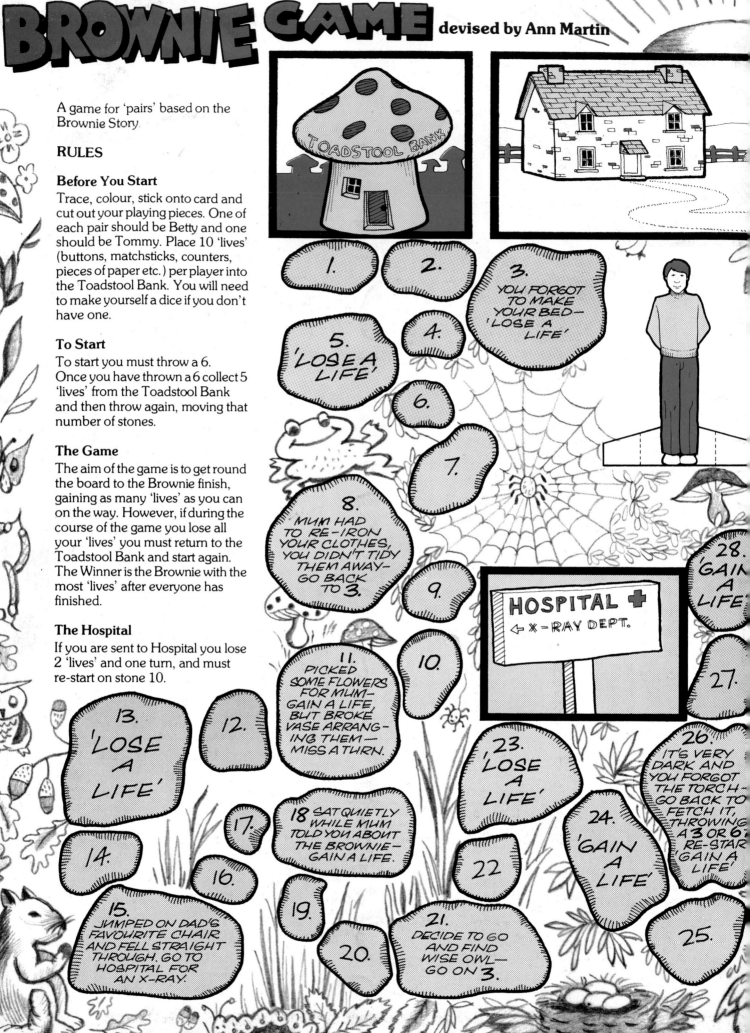

A game for 'pairs' based on the Brownie Story.

## RULES

### Before You Start
Trace, colour, stick onto card and cut out your playing pieces. One of each pair should be Betty and one should be Tommy. Place 10 'lives' (buttons, matchsticks, counters, pieces of paper etc.) per player into the Toadstool Bank. You will need to make yourself a dice if you don't have one.

### To Start
To start you must throw a 6. Once you have thrown a 6 collect 5 'lives' from the Toadstool Bank and then throw again, moving that number of stones.

### The Game
The aim of the game is to get round the board to the Brownie finish, gaining as many 'lives' as you can on the way. However, if during the course of the game you lose all your 'lives' you must return to the Toadstool Bank and start again. The Winner is the Brownie with the most 'lives' after everyone has finished.

### The Hospital
If you are sent to Hospital you lose 2 'lives' and one turn, and must re-start on stone 10.

TOADSTOOL BANK

HOSPITAL ✚
← X-RAY DEPT.

1.

2.

3. YOU FORGOT TO MAKE YOUR BED — 'LOSE A LIFE'

4.

5. 'LOSE A LIFE'

6.

7.

8. MUM HAD TO RE-IRON YOUR CLOTHES, YOU DIDN'T TIDY THEM AWAY — GO BACK TO 3.

9.

10.

11. PICKED SOME FLOWERS FOR MUM — GAIN A LIFE, BUT BROKE VASE ARRANGING THEM — MISS A TURN.

12.

13. 'LOSE A LIFE'

14.

15. JUMPED ON DAD'S FAVOURITE CHAIR AND FELL STRAIGHT THROUGH. GO TO HOSPITAL FOR AN X-RAY.

16.

17.

18. SAT QUIETLY WHILE MUM TOLD YOU ABOUT THE BROWNIE — GAIN A LIFE.

19.

20.

21. DECIDE TO GO AND FIND WISE OWL — GO ON 3.

22.

23. 'LOSE A LIFE'

24. 'GAIN A LIFE'

25.

26. IT'S VERY DARK AND YOU FORGOT THE TORCH — GO BACK TO FETCH IT, THROWING A 3 OR 6, RE-START 'GAIN A LIFE'

27.

28. 'GAIN A LIFE'